Lamb of God

Jesus' Atonement for Sin

A Devotional Bible Study and Meditation on the Sacrifice of Christ for our Sins

and Commentary for Personal Devotional Use, Small Groups or Sunday School Classes, and Sermon Preparation for Pastors and Teachers

JesusWalk® Bible Study Series
by Dr. Ralph F. Wilson
Director, Joyful Heart Renewal Ministries

Additional books, and reprint licenses are available at:
www.jesuswalk.com/books/lamb.htm

Participant Guides for free duplication are available online at
www.jesuswalk.com/lamb/lamb_lesson_handouts.pdf

JesusWalk® Publications
Loomis, California

Paperback
ISBN-13: 978-0-9832310-0-4
ISBN-10: 0983231001

Library of Congress Control Number:

Library of Congress subject headings:
    Jesus Christ – Person and offices.
    Jesus Christ – Crucifixion.
    Sacrifice – Christianity.
    Sacrifice – Biblical teaching.
    Atonement – Biblical teaching.

Suggested Classifications
    Dewey Decimal System: 232.21
    Library of Congress: BT202

Published by JesusWalk® Publications, P.O. Box 565, Loomis, CA 95650-0565, USA.

JesusWalk is a registered trademark and Joyful Heart is a trademark of Joyful Heart Renewal Ministries.

Unless otherwise noted, all the Bible verses quoted are from the New International Version (International Bible Society, 1973, 1978), used by permission.

110210

Preface

When John was preaching repentance and the forgiveness of sins while baptizing in the Jordan River, Jesus came to meet him and be baptized. John looks at him and says, "Behold, the Lamb of God, who takes away the sin of the world." In these words he capsulizes the mission of Jesus and gives us a clue to understanding the significance of Jesus' death and resurrection. In this five-week series we'll study the concept of Jesus as our atoning sacrifice for sin. As you study you'll be amazed and thankful – and a more thoughtful and faithful disciple as a result.

This study can be used a number of ways. Individual laypersons who want a serious study Christ's atonement for sin will find lots of materials to help them grow in their faith. Each lesson contains the text from the New International Version (NIV), an exposition of the passage, four or five discussion questions for thought, writing, or discussion with another person, a prayer, one or two key verses from the passage for meditation or memorization, and references I used in the study. Bible study leaders can use this book as the basis for a small group discussion, with discussion questions for each lessons included in an Appendix for copying and distribution. Pastors and teachers will find a great deal of material to serve as grist for lessons and sermons.

I also want to thank the just under 2,000 participants from 68 countries who studied these lessons with me on the Internet during the Spring of 2003. Their inspiring comments and insights make this kind of study worthwhile. I also owe a debt of thanks to the members of my adult Sunday school class for their stimulating thoughts and ideas.

This book can be used with a DVD for use in classes and small groups. At each discussion question, the group is encouraged to pause the DVD, discuss the question, and then resume the DVD to hear the next part of the lesson.

This book can be used as the Leader's Guide. The leader can make copies of each week's questions for participants, available in Appendix 5 in this book at no additional charge or online in 8.5 x 11" format at

www.jesuswalk.com/lamb/lamb_lesson_handouts.pdf

The DVD may be ordered at

www.jesuswalk.com/books/lamb.htm

I hope you find these materials useful.

Dr. Ralph F. Wilson
February 15, 2011

Copy Pricing Policy

Copying the Handouts. In some cases, small groups or Sunday school classes would like to use these notes to study this material. That's great. An appendix provides copies of handouts designed for classes and small groups. There is no charge whatsoever to print out as many copies of the handouts as you need for participants.

All charts and notes are copyrighted and must bear the line: "Copyright © 2011, Ralph F. Wilson. All rights reserved. Reprinted by permission."

You may not resell these notes to other groups or individuals outside your congregation. You may, however, charge people in your group enough to cover your copying costs.

Copying the book (or the majority of it) in your congregation or group, you are requested to purchase a reprint license for each book. A Reprint License, $2.50 for each copy is available for purchase at

www.jesuswalk.com/books/lamb.htm

Or you may send a check to:

Dr. Ralph F. Wilson
JesusWalk Publications
PO Box 565
Loomis, CA 95650, USA

The Scripture says,

"The laborer is worthy of his hire" (Luke 10:7) and "Anyone who receives instruction in the word must share all good things with his instructor" (Galatians 6:6).

However, if you are from a third world country or an area where it is difficult to transmit money, please make a small contribution instead to help the poor in your community.

Table of Contents

Abbreviations and References

ABD
The Anchor Bible Dictionary, David Noel Freedman (Editor-in-Chief) (Doubleday, 1992, 6 volumes)

BDAG
A Greek-English Lexicon of the New Testament and Other Early Christian Literature by Walter Bauer and Frederick William Danker, (Third Edition; based on a previous English edition by W.F. Arndt, F.W. Gingrich, and F.W. Danker; University of Chicago Press, 1957, 1979, 2000)

BDB
A Hebrew and English Lexicon of the Old Testament, by Francis Brown, S.R. Driver, and Charles A. Briggs (Clarendon Press, 1907)

DJG
Dictionary of Jesus and the Gospels, Joel B. Green, Scot McKnight, and I. Howard Marshall (editors), (InterVarsity Press, 1992)

DLNT
Dictionary of the Later New Testament, edited by Ralph P. Martin and Peter H. Davids (InterVarsity Press, 1997), ISBN 0830817794.

DNTB
Dictionary of New Testament Background, edited by Craig A. Evans and Stanley E. Porter (InterVarsity Press, 2000)

DOTP
Dictionary of the Old Testament Pentateuch, edited by T. Desmond Alexander and David W. Baker (InterVarsity Press, 2003)

Jeremias, *Eucharistic Words*
Joachim Jeremias, *The Eucharistic Words of Jesus* (Oxford: Basil Blackwell, 1955; translated from the second German edition by Arnold Ehrhardt)

ISBE   *The International Standard Bible Encyclopedia*,
            Geoffrey W. Bromiley (general editor), (Eerdmans,
            1979-1988; fully revised from the 1915 edition)

KJV   King James Version (1611)

Marshall,   I. Howard Marshall, *Last Supper and Lord's Supper*
Last   (Eerdmans, 1980)
Supper

Morris,   Leon Morris, *The Apostolic Preaching of the Cross*
Apostolic (Eerdmans, 1955)
Preaching

NIDNTT   *The New International Dictionary of New Testament
            Theology*, Colin Brown (general editor), (Zondervan,
            1975-1978; translated with additions and revisions
            from *Theologisches Begriffslexikon zum Neuen Testament*,
            1967-1971, three volume edition).

NRSV   *New Revised Standard Version* (Division of Christian
            Education, National Council of Churches of Christ in
            the USA, 1989)

NIV   *New International Version* (International Bible
            Society, 1973, 1978, 1983)

TDNT   *Theological Dictionary of the New Testament*,
            Gerhard Kittel and Gerhard Friedrich (editors),
            Geoffrey W. Bromiley (translator and editor),
            (Eerdmans, 1964-1976; translated from *Theologisches
            Wörterbuch zum Neuen Testament*, ten volume edition).

TDOT   *Theological Dictionary of the Old Testament*, G.
            Johannes Botterweck and Helmer Ringgren (eds.),
            John T. Willis (transl.), (Eerdmans, 1974-), translated

from *Theologisches Wörterbuch zum Alten Testament* (Verlag W. Kohlhammer GmbH, 1970-)

TWOT   ***Theological Wordbook of the Old Testament***, R. Laird Harris, Gleason L. Archer, Jr., and Bruce K. Waltke (editors), (2 volumes, Moody Press, 1980), ISBN: 0802486312

Young   Edward J. Young, *The Book of Isaiah* (3 volumes, originally in the New International Commentary on the Old Testament series; Eerdmans, 1972)

1. Behold, the Lamb of God: Basic Concepts of Sacrifice (John 1:29)

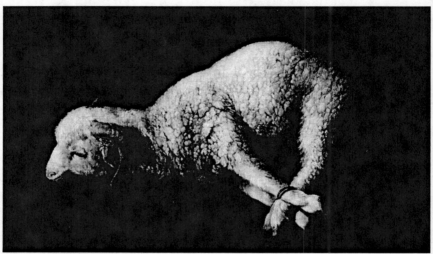

"Agnus Dei" (1635-40), Francisco de Zurburón (1598-1664), oil on canvas 38 x 62 cm., Museo Nacional del Prado, Madrid

Today we are beginning a journey of discovery, to learn what it means to call Jesus "the Lamb of God."

I hope you'll begin with an open heart and mind. Some of you have heard all this before. For others it will be brand new – and a little disturbing. My goal for us is to understand at a deeper level just who Jesus is and what he did for us – not only to understand it, but to internalize its values and commitment.

But to get to this place, we need to begin slowly and carefully. I don't want to assume that you know anything already. Nor do I want to overwhelm you. The Bible is full of literally thousands of verses bearing on the themes we'll be studying. Some of you can quote many of them from memory, but I'll be purposely resisting the temptation to give you all the cross references that prove or illustrate every point. Rather, my method will be to look deeply at a few passages of scripture. It's simpler that way for you to learn.

To begin, let's examine our theme passage.

John the Baptist's Prophetic Insight

John the Baptist is preaching a message of repentance and baptism for the forgiveness of sin. Thousands have come to him as he is baptizing along the Jordan River. One day, John speaks about the Messiah, for whom he has been sent to prepare. Now our theme verse:

> "The next day John saw Jesus coming toward him and said, 'Look, the Lamb of God, who takes away the sin of the world!'" (John 1:29)

John repeats this saying a little later (John 1:36). The context of these verses doesn't tell us a great deal about what John the Baptist actually meant when he said this. So let's examine the words themselves.

"Behold" (KJV) is the Greek particle *ide*, which can be taken two ways. (1) to point out something to which the speaker wishes to draw attention. "look! see!" and (2) to indicate a place or individual, "here is (are)."[1] So the NRSV translates John 1:29, "Here is the Lamb of God..." John draws attention to Jesus and indicates that Jesus is the focus of his words which follow. Let's look at these words one by one.

"Lamb," the Greek noun *amnos*, refers to a young sheep, including at least up to one year old.[2] In the Book of Revelation the noun *arnion* is used to designate a sheep of any age.[3]

"Of God" can mean either "sent from God" or perhaps "owned by God." John says that Jesus is in some way like a lamb sent from or provided by God himself.

[1] *Ide*, BDAG 446.
[2] *Amnos*, BDAG 54.
[3] *Arnion*, BDAG 133.

"Sin" is the common Greek noun *harmartia*. Originally it meant "to miss the mark, be mistaken." In the New Testament it occurs 173 times as a comprehensive expression of everything opposed to God.[4] Sin and forgiveness of sin are major themes of the Bible, both Old and New Testaments. Our modern society really doesn't like the concept of sin at all – though dealing with guilt is a major psychological problem that plagues people of all religions and no religion. If we are intent to understand what "Lamb of God" really means, we must be willing to discuss the forbidden "S" word – "sin."

"Of the world" employs the Greek noun *kosmos*, which refers here to "humanity in general."[5] Jesus doesn't come to deal with just a single person, or the sin of just the Jewish people for that year, but for the sins of everyone in the whole world for all time.

"Take away" describes what the Lamb will do with sin, employing the Greek verb *airō*, which means generally "to lift up and move from one place to another." Here it means "to take away, remove, blot out."[6]

"Behold, the Lamb of God, who takes away the sin of the world."

What specific lamb is John the Baptist referring to? It could be the Passover Lamb or the lamb described in Isaiah 53, or perhaps he is using it in a general sense.[7] The context doesn't help us pinpoint it further. But clearly, John indicates that Jesus is the Lamb of God in some sacrificial sense, since lambs were

---

[4] Walther Günther, "Sin," NIDNTT 3:573-583.

[5] *Kosmos*, BDAG 562.

[6] *Airō*, BDAG 28. Joachim Jeremias, *"airō,"* TDNT 1:185-186, indicates that *airo* can refer here to either the substitutionary bearing of penalty (if the Suffering Servant of Isaiah 53 is in mind) or "the setting aside of sin by the expiatory power of the death of Jesus." Jeremias prefers the latter approach.

[7] George R. Beasley-Murray, *John: Word Biblical Commentary 36* (Word, 1987), pp. 24-25; Raymond E. Brown, *The Gospel According to John* (Anchor Bible vol. 29; Doubleday, 1966), 1:58-63; C.K. Barrett, *The Gospel According to St. John* (Second Edition; Westminster Press, 1978), 175-177.

commonly used by the Jews for sacrifices to obtain forgiveness for sin. Our next step is to try to understand animal sacrifice.

Q1. (John 1:29) How do you know that John the Baptist's statement about the Lamb of God refers to sacrifice?. How was the comprehensiveness of "sin of the world" so radical a concept? http://www.joyfulheart.com/forums/index.php?showtopic=41

Ancient Animal Sacrifice

Nearly every culture throughout the world has employed sacrifice, usually animal sacrifice, to somehow appease the anger of the gods. Many moderns have dismissed this sort of appease-ment as a primitive and ignorant gesture. They are offended by the idea that blood must be shed to make atonement and have searched for other theories of the atonement that provide simpler explanations. However, to be faithful to Scripture, we can't disregard sacrifice so cavalierly. (See the Appendices for my essay "Classic Protestant Liberalism and the Atonement: A Plea for Reconsideration," "Theories of the Atonement," and a brief quote from C.S. Lewis on "Boys Philosophies")

Abraham, Isaac, and Jacob sacrificed to God as part of their worship. We don't have any indication that they were trying to "appease an angry God." That explanation is a straw man that applies better to pagan sacrifice than Jewish sacrifice. At Mt. Sinai, God gave Moses explicit instructions to build an altar of burnt offering in the tabernacle (Exodus 27), as well as rather complex instructions concerning types of sacrifices appropriate for various kinds of offences (Leviticus 1-7).

Holiness, Anger, and Justice

Yet anger must be part of our understanding. We live in a society that seeks to pull God down to its own level. But a careful reading of Exodus, Leviticus, Numbers, and Deuteronomy make it quite clear that God is to be considered holy and righteous, separate from humans and human sinfulness. Human sin, breaking of God's laws, is deeply offensive to God. Unless their sins are cleansed, humans may not even approach his holy presence.

God is angry – not at humans for their own sake – but at their sin. Anger at sin shouldn't surprise us. If your spouse lies to you, shouldn't you be angry? Sad, yes, but angry, too. If your spouse is unfaithful to you, shouldn't you be angry? Or should you be passive in the face of immorality and deceit? Moral people are outraged at sin; immoral people are calloused with regard to sin.

It's one thing to be angry, but anger must not lead to injustice. The God of the Old Testament cannot be accurately described as capricious, acting merely out of anger. Nor, for that matter, is he perpetually angry. He is described as:

> "The LORD, the LORD, the compassionate and gracious God, slow to anger, abounding in love and faithfulness, maintaining love to thousands, and forgiving wickedness, rebellion and sin. Yet he does not leave the guilty unpunished." (Exodus 34:6-7)

Q2. Why is anger an appropriate response to sin? What is the difference between capricious or uncontrolled anger and anger that brings about justice?
http://www.joyfulheart.com/forums/index.php?showtopic=42

God provides animal sacrifice as a way that justice can be done, that men and women's sins can be atoned for, and that they can approach God once more.

The Repulsiveness of Animal Sacrifice

We moderns are often repulsed by the very idea of killing an animal. The Israelites were herdsmen. Our forebears were farmers. But we city folk don't routinely butcher animals, drain out their blood, and cut them up. The closest we come is cold meat in a Styrofoam tray or butcher's wrap from the supermarket. We eat meat, for the most part, but we are insulated from the killing that is required.

Nevertheless, taking of any life should affect us as it affected the Israelites. The Israelites were very well aware that blood required taking of life.

Q3. Why is animal sacrifice repulsive to modern people? How much of this has to do with a city vs. a farming way of life?
http://www.joyfulheart.com/forums/index.php?showtopic=43

Atonement

And taking life, even to eat, is never a trivial thing. God tells Moses:

> "For the life of a creature is in the blood, and I have given it to you to make atonement for yourselves on the altar; it is the blood that makes atonement for one's life." (Leviticus 17:11)

The word translated "atonement" here is the Hebrew verb *kāpar, kipper*, "to make an atonement, make reconciliation, purge." An equivalent Arabic root means "cover" or "conceal," but evidence that the Hebrew root means "to cover over sin" is weak. Rather, the root idea of *kipper* seems to be "to purge," related to an Akkadian cognate *kuppuru* meaning "to wipe clean."[8] Our English word "atonement" comes from the Middle English "at-one-ment" or "reconciliation," which expresses the result of an atoning sacrifice. To sum up, "atonement" in Hebrew seems to mean "to wipe clean, purge," a sacrifice that cleanses from sin.

Basic Elements of Sacrifice for Sin

There were five types of sacrifices in the tabernacle (and later in the temple) – burnt offering, grain offering, peace or fellowship offering, sin (purification) offering, and guilt (reparation) offering. To comprehend the basics of sacrifice, let's look carefully at a sacrifice for purification from sin by a common person which displays the typical elements. Here a female goat or lamb (Hebrew *kebeś, keśeb*[9]) is referred to:

> "When anyone is guilty in any of these ways, he must **confess** in what way he has sinned and, as a penalty for the sin he has committed, he must bring to the LORD a female lamb or goat from the flock as a sin offering; and the priest shall make **atonement** (*kāpar*) for him for his sin." (Leviticus 5:5-6)

> "If he brings a lamb as his sin offering, he is to bring a female **without defect**. He is to **lay his hand on its head** and **slaughter it** for a sin offering at the place where the burnt offering is slaughtered. Then the priest shall **take some of the blood** of the sin offering with his finger and put it on the horns of the altar of burnt offering and pour out the rest of the blood at the base of the altar. He shall **remove all the fat**, just as the fat is removed from the lamb of the fellowship offering, and the priest shall **burn it on the altar** on top of the offerings made to the LORD by fire. In this way the priest will make atonement (*kāpar*) for him

---

[8] Richard E. Averbeck, "Sacrifices and Offerings," DOTP 706-732, especially p. 710. R. Laird Harris, *kāpar*, TWOT #1023.

[9] *Kebeś, keśeb* mean "lamb, sheep." Of the 128 occurrences, only 17 do not occur in the context of sacrifice. The root in Akkadian means "lamb," in Arabic the root refers to "young ram." TWOT #949. "Lamb" in BDB 461.

for the sin he has committed, and **he will be forgiven**." (Leviticus 4:32-35)

Here are some of the key elements of sacrifice as they appear by the time the Mosaic Law is given – simplified a bit:

1. **Confession** of the sin (5:5)
2. **Bringing an animal** that has **no defect** that might decrease its market value (4:32). It must be healthy and whole or it is not fit to offer to God. An animal like this could be rather costly, though a poor person might bring a pair of pigeons or doves instead.
3. **Lay his hands** on its head (4:33a). There seems to be a sense in which the offerer's sin is imparted to the animal through the laying on of hands (see Leviticus 16:21).
4. **Slay the animal** by cutting its throat (4:33b).
5. **Blood is collected** by a priest, put on the horns of the altar, and poured out at the base of the altar (4:34)
6. Remove the **fat portions**, which are given to the priest and **burned on the altar** (4:35). (In the case of burnt offerings, the entire animal would be burned on the altar.)
7. The **meat is eaten** by the priests in the case of a sin offering (6:24-29). (In case of a peace or fellowship offering, most of the meat would be eaten by the offerer and his family as a kind of sacred meal.)

From this analysis of a sacrifice for sin I see several principles:

1. **Confession** or acknowledgement of sin is a necessary part of the sacrifice.
2. A sacrificial animal is **costly** to the sinner. Nothing free here.
3. There is a **close identification** between the sinner and the sacrifice. The imparting of sin by the laying on of hands

suggests that the animal becomes a substitute for the sinner.

4. Killing the animal is very **personal**. It is not done *for* the
    sinner by a third party but *by* the sinner himself.

Q4. (Leviticus 4:32-35; 5:5-6) What are the basic elements involved
in a sacrifice for sin? Which of these are still necessary for
forgiveness of sins today? Which are no longer necessary? Why?
http://www.joyfulheart.com/forums/index.php?showtopic=44

Forgiveness and Grace of God

In spite of this elaborate sacrificial system, the Hebrews became
aware that all these sacrifices alone were inadequate to really
cleanse their sins. God did not "owe" them forgiveness because
they went through some ritual. Nor was God impressed or
gratified by all this killing of animals. (See Hebrews 10:8; 9:9, 13;
Psalm 50:8-12; 51:16; Isaiah 1:11-15; 66:3; Jeremiah 6:20; 7:21-22;
Hosea 6:6; Amos 5:21-22; Micah 6:6-8; Mark 12:33.)

In fact, the author of Hebrews rightly declares, "it is impossible
for the blood of bulls and goats to take away sins" (Hebrews 10:4),
for the "lesser" animal cannot really substitute for the "greater"
human being. Man needs someone greater than himself to actually
atone for and do away with sin.

There is a real sense in which God uses the sacrificial system to
teach the Jews lessons about sin, holiness, confession, forgiveness,
sin's costliness, and sin's horror. God, in his mercy, allows these

sacrifices to purge their sins, but the only fully adequate sacrifice for sin is still to come.

Behold, the Lamb of God

That is the context from which John the Baptist speaks when he says, "Behold, the Lamb of God who takes away the sin of the world" (John 1:29). Jesus is greater than our analogies, of course. But there is a sense in which the analogy of the sacrificial Lamb fits Jesus accurately, since he, as Son of God and Son of Man is the only One perfect and great enough to actually atone for sin and, at the same time, represent and substitute for all men in this atonement – once and for all.

Look! This is the Lamb of God, who takes away the sin of the world!

Prayer

Father, I'm aware again of how horrible all that killing and blood must be. It forces me to think about the horror of my own sin and rebellion against you – and the horror of sacrifice that my sins require so that I might be cleansed and stand before you forgiven. I've passed over sin, made it something trivial when it is not. Forgive me, Lord, for my sins. In the name of the Lamb of God, Jesus my Lord, I pray. Amen.

Q5. In what sense is God's provision of animal sacrifice for forgiveness of sins an expression of his mercy? Were animal sacrifices actually adequate to atone for human sin?
http://www.joyfulheart.com/forums/index.php?showtopic=45

Q6. What do you think God intended animal sacrifice teach us about sin? What do they teach us about holiness? What do they teach us about God's nature?
http://www.joyfulheart.com/forums/index.php?showtopic=46

Key Verse

"The next day John [the Baptist] saw Jesus coming toward him and said, 'Look, the Lamb of God, who takes away the sin of the world!'" (John 1:29)

2. The Lamb Who Took Our Place (Isaiah 53)

Philip the Evangelist is on the road to Gaza when the Spirit of God directs him to a chariot containing the treasurer of Ethiopia, reading and trying to make sense out of Isaiah 53:7-8:

> "He was **led like a sheep to the slaughter**, and **as a lamb** before the shearer is silent, so he did not open his mouth." (Acts 8:32-33)

He asks Philip who the prophet is talking about. Luke records, "Then Philip began with that very passage of Scripture and told him the good news about Jesus" – the Lamb of God.

In this week's lesson we'll be examining the profound

Francisco Zurbarán (Spanish painter, 1598-1664), "The Crucifixion" (1627), oil on canvas (114-5/16" x 65-3/16"), The Art Institute of Chicago.

ways in which Isaiah 53 speaks about Jesus' ministry and mission.

Universal Atonement

When John the Baptist cries out, "Behold, the Lamb of God who takes away the sin of the world" (John 1:29), we wonder just which lamb in the Bible he is referring to. Is he thinking of this "lamb led to the slaughter" in Isaiah 53? Very likely. Other lambs mentioned in the Old Testament deal with a person's sin or perhaps a national sin (see week 1). Neither the daily sacrifices in the temple nor the Passover Lamb are strictly a sin offering (see week 4). But the Suffering Servant figure of the lamb in Isaiah 53 deals with sin on a universal basis – the sins of the nations, the sins of the whole world.

Isaiah 53 is one of a series of several passages in Isaiah 40-55 (and, perhaps, Isaiah 60) that are referred to as the "Servant Songs" because they present the "Servant of Yahweh" or the "Suffering Servant" who has a special mission.[1] In the earlier Songs, the Servant is identified as the nation Israel (49:3), but in Isaiah 53 the Servant seems to be an individual rather than the nation itself. Some early Jewish commentators even saw the passage as Messianic.[2]

Notice the scope of the Servant's ministry in Isaiah 52:13 to 53:12:

"he will sprinkle **many nations**" (52:15)

"laid on him the iniquity **of us all**." (53:6)

"transgression of **my people**" (53:8)

"will justify **many**" (53:11)

"he bore the sin **of many**" (53:12)

In 53:8 the prophet focuses on the sins of the Jewish nation. But the Servant's role is broader; it clearly extends to "many nations." The Servant, depicted as a lamb in 53:7, actually "takes away the sin of the world" (John 1:29).

---

[1] The four traditional "Songs" are Isaiah 42:1-4; 49:1-6; 50:4-9 and 52:13-53:12. Some would add part of Isaiah 61 as a fifth Song. R.T. France, "Servant of Yahweh," DJG 744-747.

[2] Particularly the Targum on Isaiah 53.

In your answers to these questions, please don't just parrot your Sunday school knowledge and Bible verses. Rather, take time to dig into this text deeply and see what *it* says *itself*. You'll be richer for it.

Q1. From how large a group of people does God remove sins in Isaiah 52:13 - 53:12? In what sense is this a universal sacrifice of salvation? In what sense is Jesus' sacrifice wasted on some people? http://www.joyfulheart.com/forums/index.php?showtopic=50

Jesus Saw His Ministry as a Fulfillment of Isaiah 53

When you look at all the New Testament passages that quote or have clear allusions to Isaiah 53 (see Appendix 3), you can see that this passage has been *extremely influential* in the way that the Apostles understood Jesus' death. It's also pretty clear that this passage was at the core of how Jesus understood his own mission. Let me offer some examples that prove my point (skipping over passages where the Gospel writers themselves cite Isaiah 53 as a fulfillment):

- "...Just as the Son of Man did not come to be served, but **to serve**, and to give his life as a **ransom for many**" (Matthew 20:28=Mark 10:45). This is not a direct quotation, but a conceptual parallel. Four parallel ideas indicate that Isaiah 53 is the primary source of Jesus' teaching here: (1) the servanthood, (2) atoning death, (3) the idea of voluntarily giving one's life, and (4) the wording "for many," which parallels the words "many" (53:11) and "of many" (53:12).[3]

- In Jesus' words at the Last Supper this "for many" phrase is also repeated: "This is my blood of the covenant, which is poured out **for many** for the forgiveness of sins" (Matthew 26:28 = Mark 14:24).[4]

- "Why then is it written that the Son of Man must **suffer** much and **be rejected**?'"(Mark 9:12) – a pretty clear reference to 53:3. To his companions on the road to Emmaus, Jesus begins, "'Did not the Christ **have to suffer these things and then enter his glory**?' And beginning with Moses and all the Prophets, he explained to them what was said in all the Scriptures concerning himself." (Luke 24:25-27) This is a reference to 52:13 and 53:12. See also Mark 8:31; 9:31; 10:32-34; 14:21. Isaiah 53 provides the clearest Old Testament prediction of Messianic suffering – more than Daniel 7:13-14 and Zechariah 11-13.[5]

- Among several allusions is a direct quote of Isaiah 53:12 from Jesus' own lips: "It is written: '**And he was numbered with the transgressors**'; and I tell you that this must be fulfilled in me. Yes, what is written about me is reaching its fulfillment." (Luke 22:37).

- Finally, Jesus reads Isaiah 61:1-2 – closely related to the Servant Songs – at Nazareth (**"The Spirit of the Lord is upon me..."**) and says, "Today this scripture is fulfilled in your hearing" (Luke 4:18-21).

---

[3] France, DJG 744-747. Sydney Page, "Ransom Saying," DJG 660-662. William L. Lane, *Commentary on the Gospel of Mark* (New International Commentary on the NT series; Eerdmans, 1974), pp. 383-385. FF. Bruce, *New Testament Development of Old Testament Themes* (Eerdmans/Paternoster Press, 1968), chapter 7. More on this in Lesson 3.

[4] Lane, *Mark*, p. 507. Joachim Jeremias, *polloi*, TDNT 6:536-545, especially pp. 543-545. France, DJG 746.

[5] Also in Numbers 5:7-8; 6:12; 18:9; 1 Samuel 6:3-4, 8, 17; 2 Kings 12:16; Ezekiel 40:39; 42:13; 44:29; 46:20.

Jesus obviously knew the Servant Songs well and was convinced that they spoke about his own mission and destiny.

Q2. Which New Testament parallels to Isaiah 53 convince you that Jesus himself saw his own mission and destiny spelled out in Isaiah 53? If you aren't convinced, what stands in your way? http://www.joyfulheart.com/forums/index.php?showtopic=51

Isaiah 53 is a complex passage. My approach won't be a verse-by-verse commentary, but a topical study of five themes which relate to Jesus' work of atonement.

1. The Servant Is a Substitute Who Bears Our Sin

The first clear theme on atonement is that the Servant – or Lamb, in our analogy – is more than a helper, advisor, or victor. He is a substitute for us, that is, he bears our sins instead of us. Consider these verses:

- "Surely he **took up** (*nāśā'*) our infirmities and **carried** (*sābal*) our sorrows, yet we considered him stricken by God, smitten by him, and afflicted. But he was pierced **for** our transgressions, he was crushed **for** our iniquities..." (53:4-5)
- "...the LORD has **laid on** (*pâga'*) him the iniquity of us all." (53:6)
- "...the LORD makes his life a **guilt offering** (*'āshem*) ..." (53:10)

- "... he will **bear** (*sābal*) their iniquities." (53:11)
- "For he **bore** (*nāśā'*) the sin of many and made **intercession** (*pâga'*) for the transgressors." (53:12)

At the risk of being too technical, I'd like you to dip into the original Hebrew to see exactly what is meant, though most of the Hebrew words in Isaiah 53 will be explained only in the footnotes.

In 53:10 we find the Hebrew noun is *'āshem,* which means "guiltiness, offering for sin, sin, trespass, trespass offering." With few exceptions, this noun denotes the "trespass offering" (KJV) or "guilt offering" (NRSV, NIV), and occurs 22 times in Leviticus.[6] In several of these instances a lamb is the guilt offering (Leviticus 14:13, 21, 24-25; Numbers 6:12).[7] Clearly the Servant – the Lamb – is seen as a trespass offering, but one who takes the sin of not just a few, but all.

Now let's look at three key verbs, each repeated twice within the larger passage:

- *nāśā'* – "lift, carry, take." The term is used literally, as well as figuratively "of bearing the guilt or punishment of sin," such as in Genesis 4:13; Leviticus 5:1, 17; 7:18; Numbers 5:31; 14:34; Leviticus 10:17. The word is used of the scapegoat bearing Israel's sins into the wilderness on the Day of Atonement (Leviticus 16:22). *Nasa'* can also imply "the taking away, forgiveness, or pardon of sin, iniquity, and

---

[6] G. Herbert Livingston, *'āsham,* TWOT #180b. Diether Kellermann, *"'asham,"* TDOT 1:429-437. Kellermann sees *'ashem* in Isaiah 53:10 as "the vicarious suffering of the righteous is the guilt-offering for the many. Like a guilt-offering, the death of the Servant results in atonement, the salvation of sinners from death." Joachim Jeremias, *"pais theou,"* TDNT 5:654-717, offers a thorough discussion of Isaiah 53, especially his section on "The Suffering Servant of God in Deutero-Isaiah," pp. 666-673. Notes that his suffering is vicarious, p. 671, fn. 98 noting the use of the common sacrificial term *'asham* in 53:10 and the use of the image of the slaughtered animal.

[7] Walter C. Kaiser, *nāśā',* TWOT #1421. Young, *Isaiah* 3:345 and fn. 14.

transgression" (Exodus 34:7; Numbers 14:18; Micah 7:18; Psalm 32:1, 5).[8]

- *sābal* – The primary meaning is "bear, transport (such as a heavy load)" with "stress on the process of bearing or transporting a load (Isaiah 46:7), hence becomes a figure of servitude (Genesis 49:15)." In Isaiah 53 it puts the stress of bearing the weight of man's sickness, sorrows, sin, and punishment.[9] I wonder how heavy this load of sin felt when it settled in upon Jesus?
- *pâga'* – In the Hiphil tense there are two primary meanings, both used in our text – "to intercede" (Isaiah 53:12) and "to lay, burden" (Isaiah 53:6).[10]

So the Servant-Lamb in this passage carries or bears the heavy load of sin, as would a sacrifice. But it is *our* sin – the sin of all of us – that is laid upon him.

In Lesson 1 we studied the idea of transfer from the sinner to the sacrifice by means of the laying on of hands. The sin is understood to pass from the sinner to the sacrifice which then carries the sins. There is a strong conceptual parallel – though not a verbal parallel – to Isaiah 53 found in the Apostle Paul's Second Letter to the Corinthians:

> "God made him who had no sin **to be sin for us**, so that in him we might become the **righteousness** of God." (2 Corinthians 5:21)

You must admit, it's a pretty awe-inspiring concept – that our sins transfer to him, and his righteousness to us. Another New

---

[8] R.D. Patterson, *sābal*, TWOT #1458.

[9] Victor B. Hamilton, *pâga'*, TWOT #1731.

[10] Hebrew verb *nāga'*– the root idea of *nāga'* is "to touch, to contact." Here it has the idea of "inflicting a blow upon." The closely-related noun *nega'* refers to a physical blow or to the punishment an overlord gives a subject – sometimes what a father gives his son as proper punishment, sometimes of God as the Father who inflicts punishment. (Leonard J. Coppes, *nāga'*, TWOT #1293 and #1293a).

Testament passage, this time from Peter, is in some ways a paraphrase of Isaiah 53 that clearly points out the atoning work of Christ:

> "To this you were called, because **Christ suffered for you**, leaving you an example, that you should follow in his steps.
>   **"He committed no sin,**
>   **and no deceit was found in his mouth."** [quotes Isaiah 53:9]
> When they hurled their insults at him, he did not retaliate; when he suffered, he made no threats. Instead, he entrusted himself to him who judges justly. He himself **bore our sins** in his body on the tree, so that we might die to sins and live for righteousness; **by his wounds you have been healed** [quotes Isaiah 53:5]. For you were **like sheep going astray**, but now you have returned to the Shepherd and Overseer of your souls." (1 Peter 2:24-25)

Notice, the phrase "by his wounds you have been healed"? This moves us to our second theme....

2. The Servant Is a Substitute Who Bears Our Punishment

Besides bearing the sins of the people, the Servant in Isaiah also bears their punishment, standing in as a substitute in their place. Notice the verbs that indicate the punishment he undergoes from both God and man:

- "... we considered him stricken (*nāga'*) by God, smitten (*nākâ*[11]) by him, and afflicted (*'ānâ*[12])." (53:4)
- "He was oppressed (*nāgaś*[13]) and afflicted (*'ānâ*)..." (53:7)

---

[11] Hebrew verb *nākâ*, "smite, strike, hit, beat, slay, kill." Sometimes God is the subject of *nākâ*, bringing judgment (Marvin R. Wilson, *nākâ*, TWOT #1364).

[12] Hebrew verb *'ānâ*, The primary meaning is "to force," or "to try to force submission," and "to punish or inflict pain upon" (Leonard J. Coppes, *'ānâ*, TWOT #1652).

[13] Hebrew verb *nāgaś*, "exact, exert demanding pressure" The root connotes "the exertion of demanding oppressive pressure for payment or labor" (Leonard J. Coppes, *nāgaś*, TWOT #1296).

- "Yet it was the LORD's will to crush (*dākā'*[14]) him and cause him to suffer (*chālâ*[15]) ..." (53:10)

Two verses bring out especially clearly the idea that he bears punishment on our behalf – the Servant in exchange for sinners:

"But he was pierced (*chālal*[16]) **for our transgressions,**
he was crushed (*dākā'*) **for our iniquities**;
the punishment (*mûsār*) that **brought us peace** (*shālôm*) was
upon him,
and by his wounds (*chabbûrâ*[17]) **we are healed** (*rāpā'*[18])." (53:5)

"For the transgression **of my people** he was stricken (*nega'*)." (53:8)

The key word for this "punishment" is the Hebrew noun *mûsār*, "discipline," which normally notes "correction which results in education."[19] But E.J. Young observes that *mûsār* does not mean "instruction" in this context. "It is rather a chastisement

---

[14] Hebrew verb *dākā'* means "be crushed, contrite, broken." God crushes the oppressor (Psalm 72:4) and the wicked (Job 34:25), but not the prisoner (Lamentations 3:34). (Herbert Wolf, *dākā*, TWOT #427). Young, *Isaiah* 3:347 fn. 21, "crushed, broken in pieces, shattered."

[15] Hebrew verb *chālâ*, "be or become sick, weak, diseased, grieved, sorry." In 53:10 it is used in the sense of mental anguish, but could be in the physical sense, "he has wounded him" (Carl Philip Weber, *chālâ*, TWOT #655).

[16] Hebrew verb *chālal*, "wound (fatally), bore through, pierce" (Donald J. Wiseman, *chālal*, TWOT #660. Young, *Isaiah* 3:347 fn. 20).

[17] Hebrew noun *chabbûrâ*, "stripe, blow, stroke" (Gerard van Groningen, *chābar*, TWOT #598g. BDB 289). This relatively rare word is also used in Genesis 4:23; Exodus 21:25, Isaiah 1:6; Psalm 38:6; Proverbs 20:30. A related noun *chăbarbūrâ* refers to the stripes on a panther (Jeremiah 13:23). NRSV renders Isaiah 53:5 as "bruises."

[18] Hebrew verb *rāpā'* means "heal, make healthful." Often it is used figuratively of healing and forgiveness, often of an affliction that the Lord has brought upon them. Exodus 15:26; Deuteronomy 32:39; Isaiah 6:10;19:22; 57:18-19; Hosea 6:1; 7:1; 11:3; Jeremiah 3:22; 8:22; 30:17; 33:6; Psalm 6:2; 30:2; 103:3; 2 Chronicles 7:14; 30:20 (William White, *rāpā*, TWOT #2196). The root seems to mean "repair by stitching, darn, mend (BDB 950-951).

[19] Paul R. Gilchrist (*mûsār*, TWOT #877b) sees Isaiah 53:5 in the context of substitutionary atonement, with the Servant taking "the severe punishment" vicariously.

in which an evil was inflicted upon the servant, and as a result of which he has procured God's peace for us."[20]

We have sinned and deserve punishment. But we cannot stand the punishment we deserve. So the Servant-Lamb steps in to take our punishment. He takes it and takes it until it kills him – on our behalf.

You and I have questions on how this could happen. Is this fair? How can *one* person be allowed to take *another's* sin and punishment? You can find some of the answers in the Old Testament ideas of leaders who represent nations, Adam who represents the human race, etc. (Romans 5:12-21; 1 Corinthians 15:20-23). Theologians sometimes call this concept "federal headship" and have argued about it over the centuries. But whether or not we can quite understand it, Isaiah 53 is pretty clear that the Servant-Lamb does indeed take our sin and punishment upon him, and the New Testament is unanimous that because of this we are forgiven.[21]

Q3. Isaiah 53 teaches what theologians call "the substitutionary atonement." In what sense does the Servant act as a substitute to bear our *sins*? Put it in your own words.
http://www.joyfulheart.com/forums/index.php?showtopic=52

---

[20] Young, *Isaiah* 3:348.
[21] G.N.M. Collins, "Federal Theology," *Evangelical Dictionary of Theology* (Baker, 1984), pp. 413-414.

Q4. In addition to our *sins*, the Servant also bears the *punishment* deserved by sinners. In what sense, if any, did Jesus bear the punishment due you when he died on the cross? http://www.joyfulheart.com/forums/index.php?showtopic=53

3. The Servant Acts Willingly

The third point I want you to see in Isaiah 53 is that the Servant acts willingly, voluntarily. He is not a victim, but a willing participant. The prophecy makes that clear in several ways. Notice the active verbs showing the action of the Servant:

- "... he **poured out** (*ārâ*[22]) his life unto death...." (53:12)
- "Surely he **took up** (*nāśā'*) our infirmities and **carried** (*sābal*) our sorrows..." (53:4)[23]
- "He was oppressed (*nāga'*) and afflicted (*'ānâ*) yet **he did not open his mouth**; he was led like a lamb to the slaughter (*tebach*[24])." (53:7)
- "... As a sheep before her shearers is silent, so **he did not open his mouth**." (53:7)

---

[22] The Hebrew verb is *'ārâ*, with the root idea to lay bare, uncover, expose nakedness. It is used as a figure of death with the idea "to empty, to pour out" in here and in Psalm 141:8 – "leave not my soul destitute" (KJV), "do not give me over to death" (NIV), "do not leave me defenseless" (NRSV) (Ronald B. Allen, *'ārâ*, TWOT #1692).

[23] For the verbs *nāśā'* and *sābal*, see the section in the text above under the heading, "The Servant is a Substitute Who Bears Our Sin."

[24] The Hebrew noun *tebach* means "slaughter, slaughtering." The verb and noun are mainly used to represent people as the slaughter victim, especially by God's just and terrible judgment on those who refuse to respond to his call. Psalm 44:22; Isaiah 14:21; 34:2; 65:12; Ezekiel 21:10, 11, 14, 22, 28; Jeremiah 12:13; 50:27 (Ralph H. Alexander, *tābach*, TWOT 686a).

- "After the **suffering** (*'āmāl*[25]) of his soul, he will see the light of life and be satisfied..." (53:11)

An unwilling victim would cry out and complain. Jesus did neither, but was silent before his judges and executioners. *He* poured out his soul/life unto death. *He* carried our infirmities and sorrows – because he wanted to.

4. The Servant Acts as a Priest

Now consider a fourth theme. In most of the references in this passage the Servant is a sacrifice who bears the sin and punishment due us. But in two rather remarkable verses he also appears to act as would a priest:

- "... so will he sprinkle (*nāzâ*) many nations." (52:15)
- "By his knowledge my righteous (*tsaddîq*) servant will justify (*tsādēq*) many..." (53:11)

The Hebrew verb *nāzâ* "signifies a spattering or sprinkling of blood, oil, or water, either with one's finger (Leviticus 4:6) or a 'sprinkler' (vessel, Leviticus 14:7)" and occurs 24 times in the Old Testament, nearly always as a technical term in the context of priestly action to cleanse from sin to obtain ritual purity.[26] The paradox of this passage is that though the disfigured servant is

---

[25] The Hebrew noun *'āmāl*, "labor, toil, trouble, mischief, sorrow, travail, pain, grievance." "*'Amal* relates to the unpleasant factors of work and toil" (Ronald B. Allen, *'amal*, TWOT #1639a).

[26] *Nāzâ*, TWOT #1335. Sprinkling is used in ordination, that is, purification and consecration to divine service. So Young 3:338. The Greek Septuagint reads 52:15a as "so will many nations marvel at him" (NIV) footnote. The NRSV translates the verb as "startle" with the footnote, "Meaning of Hebrew uncertain." Keil and Delitzsch 2:307-309 acknowledge that the Hebrew verb means "sprinkle," but sees the usage as unique. They note that the root of *nāzâ* signified primarily "to leap or spring" and that the cognate Arabic *naza* uses this verb to apply to the springing or leaping of living beings, caused by excess of emotion.

seen by others as unclean, yet he is the one who is offering cleansing to the nations as would a priest.

Isaiah 53:11 uses two related words – "righteous" and "make righteous." An upright priest will make sinners righteous by his sacrifices of atonement. But the righteous Servant who has borne sin, now acts as a priest to justify others. The Hiphil tense of *tsādēq* has the causative sense, "declare righteous, justify."[27] Here is the Old Testament basis of Paul's insight into justification by faith outlined in Romans 3, especially verses 24-26.

> "... and all are justified freely by his grace through the **redemption** that came by Christ Jesus. God presented him as a **sacrifice of atonement**, through faith in his blood. He did this to demonstrate his **justice**, because in his forbearance he had left the sins committed beforehand unpunished – he did it to demonstrate his **justice** at the present time, so as to be **just** and the one who **justifies** those who have faith in Jesus. (Romans 3:24-26)

In Isaiah 53 we see the Servant-Lamb as the One who justifies. In the New Testament justifying sinners is clearly a divine act (Romans 3:30; 4:5; 8:33; Galatians 3:8, 11).

5. The Servant Is Exalted by God

A final theme in Isaiah 53 I want to highlight is God's exultation of his righteous Servant.

- "See, my servant will act wisely; **he will be raised and lifted up and highly exalted**." (52:13)
- "Therefore **I will give him a portion among the great**, and he will divide the spoils with the strong..." (53:12)

In an early Christian hymn, Paul echoes this theme:

---

[27] The Hebrew verb *tsādēq* has a root meaning of "be just, righteous." The related adjective, *tsaddîq*, is used in 53:11 to describe Yahweh's Servant as "righteous." Though he bore sin, yet he himself is righteous before God. BDB 842-843; Harold G. Stigers, *tsādēq*, TWOT #1879.

> "Therefore God exalted him to the highest place
> and gave him the name that is above every name,
> that at the name of Jesus every knee should bow,
> in heaven and on earth and under the earth,
> and every tongue confess that Jesus Christ is Lord,
> to the glory of God the Father." (Philippians 2:9-11)

The Servant is vindicated and exalted publicly (see Acts 2:33; 3:13, 26). As I studied Isaiah 53 I was amazed to find that this exaltation seems to include resurrection from the dead.

> "After the suffering (*'amal*) of his soul,
> **he will see the light of life and be satisfied**..." (53:11)

The phrase "light of life" (NIV) doesn't occur in the Masoretic Hebrew text, but is found in both the Greek Septuagint translation as well as the Hebrew text of the Isaiah scroll found among the Dead Sea Scrolls.[28] The Servant's contemporaries saw him as "cut off from the land of the living" (53:8). But 53:11 indicates that the Servant will see "light" – that is, life outside the grave – even *after* his atoning death. I expect that Jesus also saw this promise, which underlies his teaching to his disciples that "it is written" that the Son of Man would be raised from the dead (Luke 24:25-27; 8:31; 9:31; 10:32-34; 14:21).

---

[28] This verse can be construed in various ways. The Masoretic Text which underlies the KJV does not include the Hebrew noun *'or*, "light" (NRSV) or "light of life" (NIV) which appears in the Septuagint and in the Dead Sea Scrolls, where light can symbolize general "life" (Herbert Wolf, TWOT #52). On Psalm 36:10, Mitchell Dahood (*Psalms* (Anchor Bible; Doubleday) 1:221-222) argues that "to see light" is often really to see the light of God's face in immortality, though this may refer to mortal life as perhaps Psalm 49:19 (so Peter C. Craigie, *Psalms 1-50* (Word Biblical Commentary vol. 19; Word, 1983), p. 292) See a similar idea in Psalm 17:15.

Q5. Which single New Testament passage best sums up for you the lessons of Isaiah 53? Why did you chose this passage? (Select from Matt. 26:38-42; Luke 22:37; John 1:29; Romans 3:24-26; 2 Cor 5:20-21; 1 Peter 2:24-25; 1 Peter 3:18; Philippians 2:5-11 – or any other passage you can think of.)
http://www.joyfulheart.com/forums/index.php?showtopic=54

After this survey of five themes in Isaiah 53, you can see why the concepts in this passage lie at the root of much of the Christian understanding of atonement. The Servant-Lamb in Isaiah 53:

1. Bears our sin as a substitutionary atonement,
2. Receives the punishment due to us on account of our sin,
3. Acts voluntarily as a sacrifice for us,
4. Performs the cleansing and justifying roles of a priest, and
5. Is finally exalted and vindicated by God in resurrection from the dead.

Who is the Lamb of God who takes away the sin of the world? Jesus. Have you asked him to take away your sin?

Prayer

Father, as I have studied Isaiah 53 I must say I am awed. I've read this before, but I guess I never really appreciated all Jesus did on my behalf – as a sacrifice, as a lamb, as a servant. Thank you, Father, for your love that prompted this amazing and ultimate act of love. In Jesus' name, I pray. Amen.

Dear friend, if you're not sure if you've ever really put your trust in Jesus before, why don't you do it right now – no matter what your religious background. Formulate a simple prayer to God and speak it out loud. Tell God that you believe in Jesus. That you have sinned. That you ask for forgiveness and cleansing. That you believe that Jesus was sacrificed for all your sins. That you'll seek to follow Jesus for the rest of your life. Conclude your prayer with thanks for God's great gift to you. If you've prayed this simple "sinner's prayer" for the first time please e-mail me and tell me what God has done for you. I'd like to have some special materials sent to you to help you in this new spiritual step you've taken. pastor@joyfulheart.com

Key Verses

"But he was pierced for our transgressions,
he was crushed for our iniquities;
the punishment that brought us peace was upon him,
and by his wounds we are healed.
We all, like sheep, have gone astray,
each of us has turned to his own way;
and the LORD has laid on him
the iniquity of us all." (Isaiah 53:5-6)

3. The Lamb Who Redeems Us from Slavery (1 Peter 1:18-19)

So far in our study of the Lamb of God we've looked at basic ideas of sacrifice (Lesson 1) and then specifically at the concept of substitutionary atonement by the Suffering Servant of Isaiah 53 (Lesson 2). This week we'll examine the theme of ransom and redemption of slaves.

Of course, the ideas of redemption and ransom are not separate from the themes of sacrifice, the Passover Lamb, and the Servant of Isaiah 53 – they are quite interwoven – but I think you'll find it valuable to trace the

El Greco (1541-1614), "Christ Carrying the Cross" (ca. 1580), oil on canvas, 41-5/16" x 31-1/8", Metropolitan Museum of Art, New York.

role of the Lamb of God as a Redeemer, one who sets the slaves free. Here is one of our theme verses:

> "For you know that it was not with perishable things such as silver or gold that you were **redeemed** from the empty way of life handed down to you from your forefathers, but with the precious blood of **Christ, a lamb** without blemish or defect." (1 Peter 1:18-19)

Slavery in the Ancient World

We live in a world where slavery is nearly abolished. But in the ancient world of the Old and the New Testaments, slavery was all too prevalent. One way to define slavery is involuntary servitude, subjecting one person to the power of another. Most slaves were considered chattel, that is, property that can be bought or sold.

Slavery came about through warfare, piracy, brigandage, the international slave trade, kidnapping, infant exposure, failure to pay a debt, forced labor of alien populations, natural reproduction of the existing slave population, and the punishment of criminals to the mines or gladiatorial combat. Of these, warfare seems to be the main source of slaves as Roman armies expanded the empire and carried out wars to reinforce their control. In urban areas of Roman imperial society, the slave population was considerable – perhaps between 17% and 33%.[1] The early church itself grew largely among the slave population, so slavery is a common topic in the New Testament. But slavery had Old Testament roots as well. Slavery was part of Israel's national memory. The Hebrews were slaves in Egypt as an alien people, stripped of their rights and subjected to forced labor in building cities for Pharaoh (Exodus 1:11-14; see also 2:23).

Q1. In the New Testament world, what class of humans were freed by payment of a redemption price or a ransom? Why do you think that Jesus, Peter, and Paul used this analogy in this week's theme verses. What aspect of the Christian life does it help explain?

http://www.joyfulheart.com/forums/index.php?showtopic=56

The Old Testament Kinsman-Redeemer

Yahweh hears their cry and prepares to deliver Israel from Egypt.

---

[1] J. Albert Harrill, "Slavery," DNTB 1124-1127.

"I am the LORD, and I will bring you out from under the yoke of the Egyptians. I will free you (*nātsal*[2]) from being slaves (*'abōdâ*[3]) to them, and I will redeem (*gā'al*) you with an out-stretched arm and with mighty acts of judgment." (Exodus 6:6)

The concept of the kinsman-redeemer is firmly rooted in Israel's law and tradition, especially seen in the story of Ruth and Boaz. The Hebrew verb *gā'al* means "to redeem, avenge, revenge, ransom, and do the part of a kinsman."[4] The very strong sense of family gave kinsmen a responsibility to look out for their close relatives in areas such as:

- Marrying a brother's widow if no children have yet been born, in order to raise up children in the brother's name (a main issue in the case of Ruth and Tamar),
- Purchasing family lands that had to be sold because of poverty, in order to keep the land in the family,
- Buying the freedom of relatives who had become slaves because of debts they couldn't pay, and
- Avenging a kinsman who was murdered.

Frequently the noun *gō'ēl* and the verb *gā'al* refer to Yahweh, who acts as kinsman to the Israelites to rescue, redeem, and avenge them when they are in trouble. Another common Hebrew word for redemption is *pādâ*, "ransom, rescue, deliver. The basic meaning of the Hebrew root is to achieve the transfer of ownership from one to another through payment of a price or an equivalent substitute."[5] A third word, the noun *kōper*, "ransom,"

---

[2] Hebrew verb *nātsal*, "deliver, rescue, save, snatch away" (Milton C. Fisher, *nātsal*, TWOT #1404).

[3] Hebrew noun *''abōdâ*, "labor, service." This can refer to any type of work or service, but here refers to the bondage of Israel in Egypt (Exodus 1:14; Nehemiah 5:18; 2 Chronicles 10:4; Isaiah 14:3; Walter C. Kaiser, *'abōdâ*, TWOT #1553c).

[4] R. Laird Harris, *gā'al*, TWOT #300.

[5] William B. Coker, *pādâ*, TWOT #1734. Morris, *Apostolic Preaching*, pp. 10-20.

which we considered in lesson 2, comes from the verb *kāpar*, which means "to atone by offering a substitute."[6]

Q2. What comparisons do you see between Jesus and the role of the Old Testament type of the Kinsman-Redeemer?
http://www.joyfulheart.com/forums/index.php?showtopic=565

With this Old Testament background to the concept of slavery, redemption, and ransom, let's examine our New Testament texts.

Redeemed by the Lamb (1 Peter 1:18-19)

"For you know that it was not with perishable things such as silver or gold that you were **redeemed (Greek *lytroō*)** from the empty way of life handed down to you from your forefathers, but with the precious blood of Christ, a lamb without blemish or defect." (1 Peter 1:18-19)

The obvious analogy here is to a slave that is to be redeemed by payment of a ransom price. The keyword in this verse, "redeemed" (NIV, KJV) or "ransomed" (NRSV), is the Greek verb *lytroō*, "to free by paying a ransom, redeem," a word widely used in the First Century of the manumission or freeing of slaves or prisoners of war.[7] In the case of slaves, the *lytron* or ransom was

---

[6] R. Laird Harris, *kāpar*, TWOT #1023a. The word was thought to mean "cover," but recent research shows that the connection to the Arabic root meaning "cover" is tenuous.

[7] *Lytroō*, BDAG 606; Morris, *Apostolic Preaching*, p. 24ff. Some scholars argue that in Biblical Greek the concept of the payment of a ransom has receded and that only the concept of deliverance is primary, but Morris makes an excellent case to the contrary.

temporarily deposited in the shrine of a god, whose property the slave became by a legal fiction.[8]

Christians are ransomed from an empty "way of life" (NIV) or "conversation" (KJV), translating the Greek noun *anastrophē*, "conduct expressed according to certain principles, way of life, conduct, behavior."[9]

The author contrasts the normal monetary ransom price with this one. On the one hand, silver and gold are "perishable" (NIV, NRSV) or "corruptible" (KJV), *phthartos*, "subject to decay or destruction, perishable."[10] On the other, Christ's blood is "precious," Greek *timios*, "pertaining to being of exceptional value, costly, precious, of great worth or value."[11]

However, freedom from slavery is not the only idea in this verse. The theme of sacrifice is present, too, since the phrase "without blemish or defect" echoes the requirement that sacrifices to Yahweh must be whole and not crippled or disabled in any way – the principle being that we offer our best to God, not that which is second best or not of full value. Both Passover lambs (Exodus 12:5) and other types of tabernacle and temple offerings (Exodus 29:1; Leviticus 1:3, 10; 3:1, 6; 4:3, 23, 28, 32; etc.) had to meet this requirement. A close parallel to this idea can be found at Titus 2:12-14.

[8] J.N.D. Kelly, *The Epistles of Peter and of Jude* (Harper's NT Commentaries; Harper & Row, 1969), p. 73. Edward Gordon Selwyn, *The First Epistle of St. Peter* (Macmillan, 1946), pp. 144-145. Morris (*Apostolic Preaching*, pp. 22-52) cites a couple of First Century manumission documents found in Diessmann, *Light from the Ancient East* (London, 1927), pp. 322, and *The Oxyrhyncus Papyri* (London, 1898), I, p. 106.

[9] *Anastrophē*, BDAG 73. "Empty" (NIV), "vain" (KJV), and "futile" (NRSV) all translate the Greek adjective *mataios*, "pertaining to being of no use, idle, empty, fruitless, useless, powerless, lacking truth" (BDAG 621).

[10] *Phthartos*, BDAG 1053

[11] *Timios*, BDAG 1005-1006.

A Ransom for Many (Mark 10:44-45)

New Testament writers didn't invent the idea of Christ's death providing a ransom or redemption price. Jesus himself said it:

> "For even the Son of Man did not come to be served, but to serve, and to give his life as a ransom (*lytron*) for many." (Mark 10:44-45 = Matthew 20:28)

The idea of substitution is very clear in Mark 10:45 because of the Greek preposition *anti*, which indicates "in place of, instead of."[12] As we noted in Lesson 2, this passage carries clear echoes of Isaiah 53. Some liberal scholars argue that these could not be Jesus' own words – that they sound "too Pauline," that the early church put these words in Jesus' mouth. But such objections seem to stem from a distaste for the concept of sacrifice rather than a viable argument against the authenticity of Jesus' words.[13] There is much more that could be said about this verse, but let's move to our third theme verse.

Bought at a Price (1 Corinthians 6:19-20)

> "Do you not know that your body is a temple of the Holy Spirit, who is in you, whom you have received from God? You are not your own; you were **bought** (*agorazo*) **at a price**. Therefore honor God with your body." (1 Corinthians 6:19-20)

This passage makes it clear that Christians, like slaves, have been bought, and God now owns them. "Bought" is the Greek verb *agorazō*, "to acquire things or services in exchange for money, buy, purchase." This idea extends to persons as well: "to secure the rights to someone by paying a price, buy, acquire as property."[14] This concept is used five other times in the New Testament:

---

[12] Morris, *Apostolic Preaching*, p. 30-32.

[13] There is excellent evidence for the authenticity of the passage, outlined by William L. Lane, *The Gospel According to Mark* (New International Commentary on the NT series; Eerdmans, 1974), pp. 377-378, fn. 75; and Leon Morris, *Apostolic Preaching*, pp. 26-35.

[14] *Agorazō*, BDAG 14.

1 Corinthians 7:23	"You were bought (*agorazō*) at a price; do not become slaves of men."
Acts 20:28	"Be shepherds of the church of God, which he bought (*peripoieō*[15]) with his own blood."
2 Peter 2:1	"[False prophets deny] the sovereign Lord who bought (*agorazō*) them – bringing swift destruction on themselves."
Revelation 5:9	"And they sang a new song: 'You are worthy to take the scroll and to open its seals, because you were slain, and with your blood you purchased (*agorazō*) men for God from every tribe and language and people and nation.'"
Revelation 14:4	"[The 144,000] follow the Lamb wherever he goes. They were purchased (*agorazō*) from among men and offered as firstfruits to God and the Lamb."

Q3. (1 Corinthians 6:19-20) How should we disciples apply the principle: "You are not your own, you were bought with a price"? How should this affect our living?
http://www.joyfulheart.com/forums/index.php?showtopic=57

---

[15] The Greek verb *peripoieō* means "to gain possession of something, acquire, obtain, gain for oneself. (BDAG 804).

Elements of the Slave Ransom Analogy

We are tracing the ransomed slave analogy in this lesson. The New Testament constantly intermixes this theme with that of sacrifice and atonement for sin. Nevertheless, let's examine the ransomed slave analogy a bit further and look at each element of the analogy in the following table:

	1 Peter 1:18-19	Mark 10:45	Acts 20:28	Revelation 5:9
Slaves	"you"	"for many"	church of God	people
Form of slavery	empty way of life	-	-	-
Ransom	Christ's blood	Jesus' life	"his own blood"	Lamb's blood
One to whom the ransom is paid	-	-	-	-
One who pays the ransom	unstated	Jesus	God	Lamb

Notice that in none of these verses is the one to whom the ransom is paid explicitly identified. God is clearly the owner now, but to whom is the ransom price paid? We aren't told because the New Testament writers don't carry the analogy that far. We'll see why in a moment.

Who or What Enslaves Us?

Our key passages only hint at what we are freed from – an "empty way of life" (1 Peter 1:18). But the New Testament is quite clear on this in other passages. Jesus explained, "I tell you the truth, everyone who sins is a **slave** (*doulos*[16]) **to sin**." (John 8:34). Paul explored this theme in his letters:

- "But now that you know God – or rather are known by God – how is it that you are turning back to those weak and miserable principles? Do you wish to be **enslaved** (*douleuō*) by them all over again?" (Galatians 4:9)
- "At one time we too were foolish, disobedient, deceived and **enslaved** (*douleuō*) by **all kinds of passions and pleasures.** We lived in malice and envy, being hated and hating one another." (Titus 3:3)
- "But thanks be to God that, though you used to be **slaves** (*doulos*) **to sin**, you wholeheartedly obeyed the form of teaching to which you were entrusted." (Romans 6:17)
- "But now that you have been **set free from sin** and have become slaves (*douloō*) to God, the benefit you reap leads to holiness, and the result is eternal life." (Romans 6:22)

The slavery is to sin. We find it habitual and cannot escape, even by our best efforts. We can identify with Paul's famous cry of despair in Romans 7.

> "So I find this law at work: When I want to do good, evil is right there with me. For in my inner being I delight in God's law; but I see another law at work in the members of my body, waging war against the law of my mind and **making me a prisoner**

---

[16] *Doulos* refers to a "male slave as an entity in a socioeconomic context, slave" (BDAG 259-260). Other words in this word group include *douleuō*, "perform the duties of a slave, serve, obey" (BDAG 259), and *douloō*, "enslave, cause to be like a slave" (BDAG 260).

(*aichmalotizō*[17]) of the **law of sin** at work within my members. What a wretched man I am! Who will rescue me from this body of death? Thanks be to God – through Jesus Christ our Lord! So then, I myself in my mind am a slave (*douleuō*) to God's law, but in the sinful nature a **slave to the law of sin**." (Romans 7:21-25a)

Our sin separates us and estranges us from God and makes us easy for Satan to deceive. Our sin makes us hopelessly in debt to God, far beyond our ability to repay. Sin has captured us in two ways:

1. Sin's addictive power entraps us in continual disobedience to God, and
2. God's justice requires that this continual, habitual disobedience be punished. We are rightly under a sentence of judgment for our disobedience.

We're in very deep, way over our heads. We need to be rescued from this plight. A Savior, a Rescuer, a miracle is our only hope.

Satan Is Defeated, Not Paid Off

None of our key passages spell out clearly who receives the ransom. Since God "owns" us, the slave-ransom analogy breaks down at this point, since it God paying a ransom to God confuses the picture. That's why the Bible authors drop it there.

Surely Satan doesn't receive a ransom! Some of the early Church Fathers explored a so-called Devil Ransom Theory – but it doesn't really work.[18]

---

[17] *Aichmalotizō*, "to cause someone to become a prisoner of war, take captive" (BDAG 31-32).

[18] Because of their sin, the theory goes, people belong to Satan. God offered his Son as ransom (as "bait," say some), a ransom which Satan accepted as a bargain. But when Satan got Jesus into hell, he found he could not hold him, and Christ rose in victory on the third day. This is not the only atonement theory that this group of Church Fathers espoused. They clearly saw the ideas of substitutionary sacrifice for sins, etc. But for the slave analogy part of the

The Bible depicts Jesus' salvation as a victorious battle with the forces of evil, personified in Satan or the devil (Mark 3:24-27; Acts 26:17-18; Luke 4:18-19; Colossians 1:13-14). But nowhere in Scripture is Satan seen as the legitimate owner of sinful people. He keeps them in darkness and holds them in his deceitful power, but he is not their legitimate owner. He is a usurper and thief (cf. John 10:10), an accuser (Revelation 12:10-12).

Satan loses his power, not because he has been paid off, but because we have been forgiven. We can no longer accurately be accused of sin. When we realize that truth, we are set free (John 8:32), no longer hopeless and manipulated by lies. Paul puts it this way:

"And when you were dead in trespasses and the uncircumcision of your flesh, God made you alive together with him, when he forgave us all our trespasses, **erasing the record that stood against us** with its legal demands. He set this aside, nailing it to the cross. He **disarmed the rulers and authorities** and made a public example of them, triumphing over them in it." (Col. 2:13-15, NRSV)

We are also given a new way of pleasing God – no longer trying to obey God's law by our own flawed efforts, but by learning to live in the power of the Holy Spirit (Romans 8:1-9).

Bible's teaching on atonement, they saw Satan as the recipient of the ransom. Leon Morris, "Atonement, Theories of the," *Evangelical Dictionary of Theology* (Baker, 1984), p. 101. See also Gustaf Aulén, *Christus Victor: An Historical Study of the 3 Main Types of the Idea of Atonement* (Macmillan, 1931).

Q4. According to the slave-ransom analogy, who is the slave?
What is he enslaved by? Who offers the ransom? If Satan is
involved in the enslaving process, why isn't the ransom paid to
him? Why isn't the slave-ransom analogy spelled out completely
in the New Testament?
http://www.joyfulheart.com/forums/index.php?showtopic=58

Q5. Extra Credit: In what sense have we been set free or released
from slavery to sin? Why do we need the Holy Spirit to help us
keep this freedom? Feel free to share stories of how Christ has
freed you.
http://www.joyfulheart.com/forums/index.php?showtopic=62

Atonement for Our Sins

This theme of deliverance from slavery is powerful, teaching us
several things:

1. God is our kinsman-redeemer who takes responsibility for
    us.
2. God loves us radically. He will not let us go. He resorts to
    extreme measures to restore us to himself – even the death
    of his Son. Whatever it takes, our God will do for us. He is
    committed to us.
3. We now belong to God. What we do is not just our own
    business. We are God's.

4.   But we are love-slaves, who voluntarily, freely serve God.

The analogy of slavery and ransom finally merges into atonement for our sins.

> "For you know that it was not with perishable things such as silver or gold that you were **redeemed from the empty way of life** handed down to you from your forefathers, but with the precious blood of Christ, **a lamb without blemish or defect**." (1 Peter 1:18-19)

Prayer

Father, thank you for your awesome love that sets me free through Jesus Christ! I am still amazed when I try to think it all through. My mind is boggled some by things I don't understand, but my heart is full of love and appreciation for your great gift to me and all my brothers and sisters. Thank you! In Jesus' name, I pray. Amen.

Key Verse

> "For you know that it was not with perishable things such as silver or gold that you were redeemed from the empty way of life handed down to you from your forefathers, but with the precious blood of Christ, a lamb without blemish or defect." (1 Peter 1:18-19)

4. The Passover Lamb of Whom We Partake (1 Corinthians 5:7)

The Apostle Paul writes, "Christ, our Passover lamb, has been sacrificed" (1 Corinthians 5:7), echoing the early church's belief that Christ was a fulfillment of the Passover or Paschal lamb (from Hebrew *pesach*, "Passover").

As I study the New Testament, I am becoming more and more convinced that Jesus, too, saw himself in this role, and implies as much in his words at the Last Supper – which, it turns out, were shared in the context of an actual Passover meal. Let's explore this aspect of Christ's ministry of atonement as the Passover Lamb. To do this, we need to go back thirteen or fourteen centuries before Christ to the people of Israel when they were slaves in Egypt.

James J. Tissot, "The Signs on the Door" (1896-1900), watercolor, Jewish Museum, New York

The Plague on the Firstborn

As God begins to deliver Israel from Egypt, he sends Moses to Pharaoh with the demand, "Let my people go!" Pharaoh refuses. Following each refusal, God sends plagues of increasing severity upon Egypt, culminating with God's decree that each firstborn

son in Egypt would be slain (Exodus 11:5). But when Moses
declares God's words to Pharaoh, Pharaoh refuses to believe
them.

To protect from this plague the Israelites who lived in Egypt,
God instructs Moses that each household should select a yearling
male lamb and slaughter it at dusk on the 14th day of Abib (the
Hebrew month that corresponds with March-April).

> "Then they are to take some of the blood and put it on the sides
> and tops of the doorframes of the houses where they eat the
> lambs" (Exodus 12:7).

During the night the angel of death passes through Egypt
slaying the firstborn of both men and animals to bring judgment
on Pharaoh and the gods of Egypt.

> "The blood will be a sign for you on the houses where you are;
> and when I see the blood, I will pass over (*pasach*) you. No
> destructive plague will touch you when I strike Egypt" (Exodus
> 12:13).

> "When the LORD goes through the land to strike down the
> Egyptians, he will see the blood on the top and sides of the
> doorframe and will pass over (*pasach*) that doorway, and he will
> not permit the destroyer to enter your houses and strike you
> down" (Exodus 12:23)

The Hebrew verb used in these verses is *pāsach*. While there are
several theories about the meaning of this verb, two seem most
plausible. The traditional etymology is the meaning "to pass
(over),"[1] that is, the merciful passing over of a destructive power.
Some interpret *pāsach* as meaning "to defend, protect," that is,
"the Lord will protectively cover the houses of the Israelites and
will not allow the destroyer to enter."[2] In either case, the blood is
a sign to the Lord that the house that bears it should be exempted
from the judgment on the firstborn.

---

[1] *Pāsach*, BDB 820. Joachim Jeremias, *"pascha,"* TDNT 5:896-904; M.R. Wilson,
"Passover," ISBE 3:675-678.
[2] Victor P. Hamilton, *pāsach*, TWOT #1786.

The Sacrifice of the Passover Lamb

Just what kind of sacrifice is the initial Paschal lamb offered at the Exodus? It is not like the scapegoat on the Day of Atonement (Leviticus 16) or one of the morning and evening offerings (Exodus 29:38-43; Numbers 28:1-8). Most of these offerings were to atone for sin in some sense, while the commemorative sacrifice of Passover lambs in the temple each year was not considered as an atonement for sin.[3]

But what was the significance of the initial sacrifice of Passover lambs at the *first* Passover? Five offerings were performed in the tabernacle and, later, in the temple.[4] Of these, Old Testament scholar Richard Averbeck observes that the sacrifice of the Passover lamb bears some resemblance to the peace or fellowship offering. In this type of offering, a representative piece of meat is offered before the Lord and to the priests. The rest is eaten by the offerer and his family as a kind of celebration meal – similar to the celebration meal of the Passover. Averbeck also notes similarities between the original Passover act of placing blood on the doorpost and lintel and the ordination of priests, where blood is placed on the priest's ear, right thumb, and right big toe as an act of consecration (Leviticus 8:23-24). He sees the initial Passover offering as a consecration or setting apart of the people within each household who partook of the sacrifice.[5]

---

[3] Joachim Jeremias, *The Eucharistic Words of Jesus* (A. Ehrhardt (trans.); Basic Blackwell, 1955), pp. 146-147.

[4] Richard E. Averbeck, "Sacrifices and Offerings," DOTP 706-773.

[5] Richard Averbeck, telephone conversation, 3/5/03. R. Alan Cole refers to it as "apotropaic" in the sense of averting God's "stroke." R. Alan Cole, *Exodus* (Tyndale Old Testament Commentaries; InterVarsity Press, 1974), p. 106. "Apotropaic" means "designed to avert evil." Cole notes, "Although, strictly speaking, there is no thought of 'atonement' here, the rationale of the blood ritual is the same: it represents a life laid down (Leviticus 17:11). The term "passover sacrifice" occurs in Exodus 12:27, with similar references in Exodus 23:18 and 34:25. The Hebrew noun *zebach*, "sacrifice" is a generic noun often linked with offerings or burnt offerings. The verb *zābach* is mainly used of killing animals for sacrifice (Herbert Wolf, *zābach*, TWOT #525a).

Israel's sin doesn't seem to be in the forefront; rather, the lamb seems to be a kind of substitute or interposition for the firstborn males and animals in the household. However, there may be some idea of expiation or purification present since hyssop is used to smear the blood. Elsewhere hyssop is associated with expiation and purification.[6] In addition, some Rabbinical writings refer to the redemptive effect of the blood of the Passover lamb.[7]

Q1. (Exodus 12) In what way did the lambs on the first Passover protect the families of God's people? What is the primary point of comparison between the first Passover lambs and what Christ did for us as our Passover Lamb?
http://www.joyfulheart.com/forums/index.php?showtopic=70

The Last Supper as a Passover Meal

Jews were instructed to partake of the Passover annually to celebrate and commemorate God redeeming them from slavery in Egypt. By Jesus' day, Passover was to be celebrated only within

[6] Keil and Delitzsch, *Commentary on the Old Testament: Pentateuch*, 2:13-14, concludes that "by the smearing of the door-posts and lintel with blood, the house was expiated and consecrated on an altar." He bases this conclusion on the fact that the hyssop-bush is used, and "sprinkling with hyssop is never prescribed in the law, except in connection with purification in the sense of expiation (Leviticus 14:4, 6, 49, 51; Numbers 19:18-19; cf. Psalm 51:7)."
[7] Jeremias, *Eucharistic Words*, p. 146, n. 4, quotes *Pirqe R. 'Eli'ezer* 29 (14d): "For the merit of the blood of the covenant of the circumcision and the Passover blood, I have redeemed you out of Egypt, and for their merit you will be redeemed at the end of the fourth (Roman) universal empire (i.e., in the days of the Messiah)," cited by P. Billerbeck 4.40. *Pesahim* 10:6 reads: "May we eat there of the sacrifices and of the Passover-offerings whose blood has reached with acceptance the wall of thy Altar, and let us praise thee for our redemption and for the ransoming of our soul." (Attributed to Rabbi Akiba, early second century, quoted in Marshall, *Last Supper*, p. 168, fn. 2).

the precincts of Jerusalem, so the city was jam-packed with pilgrims during this season.

There is some question whether the Last Supper Jesus held with his disciples was a Passover meal or a special meal the day before Passover. The Synoptic Gospels are pretty clear that the Last Supper was a Passover meal (Mark 14:12; Luke 22:13-15), but the chronology of John's Gospel seems to indicate that Jesus was crucified just before Passover began (John 18:28). These can probably be harmonized by assuming the use of different calendars among the Jews.[8] However, I'm convinced that the Last Supper was indeed held on Passover as part of the Passover meal.

Let's look at some of the elements of the Passover meal as it might have been held in Jesus' day:[9] Each element of the meal was blessed and then commented upon (the *haggadah*) by the head of the household, in this case, Jesus.

- **Unleavened bread** was a symbol of past misery and the speed with which the Israelites had to pack and leave before the bread had risen (Exodus 12:34).
- **Bitter herbs** represented the bitterness of slavery (Exodus 12:8).
- **Fruit purée** was reminiscent of the clay the Israelites used to make bricks in their captivity as slaves in Egypt.
- **Passover lamb** was a reminder of God's merciful "passing over."

This was a very special meal, since neither wine nor meat were common as everyday fare. Here is a reconstruction of the meal based on the research of New Testament scholar Joachim Jeremias.[10]

[8] Marshall, *Last Supper*, pp. 57-75; Jeremias, *Eucharistic Words*, pp. 1-60.
[9] Marshall, *Last Supper*, p. 179, Table 1, copied essentially from Jeremias, *Eucharistic Words*, pp. 58-59.
[10] Jeremias, *Eucharistic Words*, p. 60.

1. **Preliminary Course**
   - Blessing of the festival day (*Kiddush*) spoken over the First Cup of wine.
   - Preliminary dish of green herbs, bitter herbs, and fruit sauce.
   - Serving of the meal proper (but not yet eating it) and mixing the Second Cup of wine.

2. **Passover Liturgy**
   - The head of the family says the Passover narrative (the *haggadah*).
   - Singing of Psalm 113 (called the "little *hallel*").
   - Drinking the Second Cup of wine.

3. **Main Meal**
   - A blessing is spoken over bread by the head of the family, who broke it and distributed it to those at the table. Here is where Jesus would have blessed the bread, broken it, and distributed to his disciples. Here he forever made the bread special and set it apart with these unique words, **"This is my body given for you. Do this in remembrance of me."**
   - Eating the meal of lamb, unleavened bread, bitter herbs.
   - Blessing spoken over Third Cup of wine, called the **Cup of Blessing** (see 1 Corinthians 10:16). Here, before the concluding "hymn," that is, the great *hallel*, Jesus would have blessed the cup and said, **"This cup is a new covenant in my blood, poured out for many (for the forgiveness of sins). Drink of it – all of you."**

4. Conclusion

- Singing of Psalms 114-118 (the called "great *hallel*"), recalling the words, "When they had sung a hymn, they went out to the Mount of Olives" (Matthew 26:30).
- Blessing spoken over the Fourth Cup of wine.

Bread and Wine in Light of the Passover Lamb

If this outline of the Passover meal at the Last Supper is accurate, then Jesus' words about the bread being his body and the cup being his blood are immediately adjacent to eating the Passover lamb. I can't escape the conclusion that Jesus' words were interpreted by his disciples – and probably intended by Jesus – to be understood in relation to the Passover and the Passover lamb.[11] Clearly the early church thought of Jesus as the Passover or Paschal Lamb that had been sacrificed (1 Corinthians 5:7). Perhaps the analogy is: Jesus interposes himself to redeem his people from their bondage to sin, just as the Passover lamb was interposed to redeem the people of Israel from slavery in Egypt.

Q2. Compare the annual Jewish Passover celebration meal in Jesus' day with the Christian's celebration of the Lord's Supper. Where are the similarities? Where are the differences?
http://www.joyfulheart.com/forums/index.php?showtopic=64

[11] Jeremias, *Eucharistic Words*, pp. 144-145.

Words of Institution Contain Explicit Sacrificial Terms (Matthew 26:26-28)

It's pretty clear that what we call Jesus' "words of institution" use clear sacrificial language.

> "While they were eating, Jesus took bread, gave thanks and broke it, and gave it to his disciples, saying, **'Take and eat; this is my body.'** Then he took the cup, gave thanks and offered it to them, saying, **'Drink from it, all of you. This is my blood of the covenant, which is poured out for many for the forgiveness of sins.'"** (Matthew 26:26-28)

The words of institution are found with some variations in Matthew 26:26-28, Mark 14:22-24; Luke 22:19-20; and 1 Corinthians 11:24-25. While I can't be exhaustive, let's briefly examine Matthew's account. Most striking to me in this passage are Jesus words: "This is my blood of the covenant, which is poured out for many for the forgiveness of sins."

1. Jesus associates the red wine with his own blood and then asks the disciples to drink it. This would be startling to anyone, especially to Jews who were prohibited from drinking blood (Leviticus 17:10-11). In John 6:53-57 such offensive words caused some disciples to leave Jesus and no longer follow him (John 6:66). Coupled with Jesus asking the disciples to eat bread that he identified as his body, we have a remarkable and powerful image. Jesus is asking his disciples to feed on him (John 6:57) and unite themselves to him and to his death using a very intimate and powerful figure. How could the disciples forget such a vivid idea? They couldn't. Jesus intended that they remember.

2. Jesus identifies his blood with the institution of a new covenant. Though the original manuscripts of Matthew's Gospel may have omitted the word "new," the concept of a new covenant was surely in his mind. The concept of the "blood of the covenant" is found in Exodus 27:7-8, where blood is sprinkled over the people of Israel when they agree to the original covenant they were making with Yahweh at the foot of Mt. Sinai. But the

Prophet Jeremiah heralded the coming of a new covenant of forgiveness of sins replacing the Mosaic covenant:

> "'The time is coming,' declares the LORD,
> 'when I will make a **new covenant**
> with the house of Israel
> and with the house of Judah...
> This is the covenant I will make with the house of Israel
> after that time,' declares the LORD.
> '... they will all know me,
> from the least of them to the greatest,' declares the LORD.
> **'For I will forgive their wickedness**
> **and will remember their sins no more.'"** (Jeremiah 31:31-34)

Q3. (Matthew 26:28) Why should the words, "This is my blood of the covenant, which is poured out for many for the forgiveness of sins" fill us with sorrow? Why should they fill us with joy?
http://www.joyfulheart.com/forums/index.php?showtopic=68

---

3. Jesus links his death with the Suffering Servant's sacrifice for the sins of many. As mentioned in Lesson 2 of this series, the phrase "for many" points back to Isaiah 53:11-12, where the Servant "bore the sin of many." Jesus uses the phrase "poured out for many for the forgiveness of sin."

To pour out blood in order to obtain forgiveness for another is clearly the concept of a blood sacrifice. In our day, some who are offended by this concept seek to reinterpret the meaning of the Lord's Supper, but it's pretty hard to hide the truth that Jesus intended it to remember his death as a sacrifice for sins.

Q4. Why is it so important to forgive those who have offended us *before* partaking of the Lord's Supper? In what sense are the Lord's Supper and unforgiveness incompatible? (Consider Matthew 26:28; 1 Corinthians 11:27; Matthew 6:14-15; 5:23-24; James 5:16.)
http://www.joyfulheart.com/forums/index.php?showtopic=67

---

4. Jesus looks forward to the ultimate Passover in the Kingdom of God.

"I tell you, I will not drink of this fruit of the vine from now on until that day when I drink it anew with you in my Father's kingdom." (Matthew 26:29)

Here Jesus is referring to the Great Banquet alluded to in both the Old and New Testaments. The Jews of Jesus' day saw this as a final or eschatological Passover celebration with Abraham, Isaac, and Jacob and the other patriarchs and prophets (Luke 13:28-29; 14:15; 22:30; Revelation 19:9)

Q5. In what way does each celebration of the Lord's Supper anticipate a future Passover meal? (Matthew 26:29; Luke 13:28-29; 14:15; 22:30; Revelation 19:9; 1 Corinthians 11:26)
http://www.joyfulheart.com/forums/index.php?showtopic=69

"Christ, our Passover lamb, has been sacrificed" (1 Corinthians 5:7), and in the Lord's Supper we are invited to partake not only of the sacrifice (see 1 Corinthians 10:16-18), but to celebrate both our redemption through Christ's atonement and his coming again. The next time you have the privilege of partaking of the Lord's Supper, remember and be thankful.

Just as the Passover lamb was interposed to redeem the people of Israel from slavery in Egypt, so Jesus interposes himself to redeem his people from their bondage to sin. Behold, the Lamb of God who takes away the sin of the world.

Prayer

Father, thank you for the rich imagery of Christ as our Passover lamb. Thank you for his willingness to be sacrificed on our behalf. Thank you for the comfort and hope that we find in the Lord's Supper. And thank you for the expectation we have of the final Banquet with you. In Jesus' name, we pray. Amen.

Key Verse

"Get rid of the old yeast that you may be a new batch without yeast – as you really are. For Christ, our Passover lamb, has been sacrificed." (1 Corinthians 5:7)

5. The Triumphant Lamb We Worship (Revelation 5:1-14)

Over the past four weeks we've been studying various aspects of atonement and redemption brought about by the Lamb of God. In this final week we examine a passage where we see some of the same themes, but with a special note of victory, joy, and finality. The suffering and pain are past and the Lamb that was slain now stands – he has been raised on high.

Detail of "Adoration of the Lamb" (1432), by Jan van Eyck, oil on wood, Ghent altarpiece, Cathedral of St. Bavo, Ghent.

An Introduction to the Book of Revelation

If you've ever read the Book of Revelation you know that it is full of symbols – beasts and elders, angels and that great serpent – all manner of interesting creatures. Some people read the Book of Revelation to figure out the time of Jesus' return. But in Chapter 5, that isn't our concern. We want to catch a glimpse of the far side of redemption. Fasten your seatbelt and take a trip with me into the heavenly throne room.

The Book of Revelation, often called the Apocalypse or the Revelation of St. John, is written by John, in exile on the Island of Patmos off the west coast of Asia Minor (modern-day Turkey). Though there are lots of theories about the author's identity, early tradition is unanimous that Revelation was written by John the Apostle, which is my tentative conclusion, as well. It was probably written late in the reign of Emperor Domitian (81-96 AD), about 95 AD. John writes of a revelation of last things shown to him by Jesus Christ (1:1).

Revelation (Greek *apocalypse*) is written in an entirely different literary style than the rest of the Bible, with the exception of parts of the Old Testament Book of Daniel. This genre, known as apocalyptic literature, includes such elements as forecasts of spiritual turmoil, mythical images rich in symbolism and composite character, and long cycles of discourse.[1] But don't mistake symbolism for uncertainty, as if the meaning is up for grabs. John uses symbols to communicate his vision of heaven and the exalted Christ, a vision that is inexpressible in human language.

The first three chapters picture the exalted Christ and give his encouragement and warnings to the seven churches of Asia. In chapter 4, John is summoned up to heaven, where he sees the throne of God surrounded by 24 elders and four living creatures. We pick up the narrative of John's vision in Chapter 5. I am resisting the temptation to comment on every element in chapter 5; I'm reserving my focus for the character and activity of the Lamb.

The Scroll with Seven Seals (5:1-4)

God on the throne holds a scroll sealed with seven seals, but no one is found worthy to break the seals and open the scroll. Scholars have debated whether this is a bound book (sometimes called a codex) or a scroll. The Greek word *biblion* could mean

[1] Dale C. Allison, Jr., "Apocalyptic," DJG 17-20.

either. Upon consideration, I think it refers to a scroll. In ancient days some legal documents (such as wills) were witnessed by seven different witnesses and each of the seven would attach his own personal seal in sealing wax, each attached to one of the seven threads wrapped around the testament. The purpose of this was to make sure that no one could open the document undetected until it was officially opened at the appropriate time. The contents of this scroll in Revelation 5 are probably either (1) a deed which conveys the promise of the kingdom of God to mankind, or (2) a testament which bestows the kingdom as God's covenant promise – which amount to the same thing. But no one is found "worthy", that is, "able" (5:6), to open the seals, since whoever opens the scroll must have the power to execute what is written in it.[2] The key question in this section is "Who is worthy?" (5.2). The Greek word is *axios*, "pertaining to being correspondingly fitting or appropriate, worthy, fit, deserving."[3] There is weeping because no one is found worthy or able.

The Lion Who Is the Lamb (5:5)

Suddenly, one of the elders says:

"See, the Lion of the tribe of Judah, the Root of David, has triumphed...." (Revelation 5:5)

About whom is he talking?

"The Lion of the tribe of Judah" refers to Jacob's ancient prophecy over his son Judah (Genesis 49:8-12), picturing Judah as "a lion's cub" and a "crouching lion," from whose tribe, the Jews believed, would come the Messiah:

"The scepter will not depart from Judah,
nor the ruler's staff from between his feet,
until he comes to whom it belongs
and the obedience of the nations is his." (Genesis 49:10)

[2] G.R. Beasley-Murray, *The Book of Revelation* (New Century Bible Commentary; Revised Edition; Eerdmans, 1978), p. 123.
[3] *Axios*, BDAG 93-94.

"The Root of David" is a reference to Isaiah's prophecy:

> "A shoot will come up from the stump of Jesse;
> from his roots a Branch will bear fruit....

> In that day the Root of Jesse will stand as a banner for the
> peoples; the nations will rally to him, and his place of rest will
> be glorious." (Isaiah 11:1, 10)

Jesse is the father of King David, from whose descendents the
Messiah would come.

Notice the verb in this sentence: "the Lion of the tribe of Judah,
the Root of David, has **triumphed**." The Greek verb is *nikaō*, "to
win in the face of obstacles, be victor, conquer, overcome,
prevail." (Nike shoes get their name from the Greek word for
victory.)[4] When Jesus said on the cross "It is finished!" (John
19:30) and was then raised from the dead on the third day, the
victory over sin and death was complete.

Q1. (Revelation 5:5) Why is the Lamb called "the Lion of the tribe
of Judah" and "the Root of David"? What do these titles signify
about him?

http://www.joyfulheart.com/forums/index.php?showtopic=71

The Slain Lamb Standing (5:6)

We expect triumph from lions, not from lambs, but when this
glorious "Lion of the tribe of Judah, the Root of David," is
announced, John sees a lamb instead. The Lion is the Lamb, an
amazing and deliberate juxtaposition of might and meekness:[5]

---

[4] *Nikaō*, BDAG 673.

[5] The lion and lamb appear together elsewhere in apocalyptic literature in the
Testament of Joseph 19:8-9 – "And all the beasts rushed against him (the lamb),

"Then I saw a Lamb, looking as if it had been slain, standing in the center of the throne, encircled by the four living creatures and the elders. He had seven horns and seven eyes, which are the seven spirits of God sent out into all the earth." (Revelation 5:6)

See what the description tells us:

- **The Lamb** is obviously a symbol for Jesus Christ himself, whom John the Baptist had proclaimed, "The Lamb of God, who takes away the sin of the world" (John 1:29). But this is no ordinary lamb.
- **Appearing to have been slain**, his wounds were visible in this vision. A sacrificial lamb would have been slain by having his throat cut. It reminds me of the line, "those wounds, yet visible above...." in the hymn "Crown Him with Many Crowns" (see below). Yet somehow, this Lamb who has been slain has triumphed – just how he has triumphed we'll see as the vision unfolds.
- **The Lamb is standing** (Greek *histēmi*, Perfect tense) in the midst of the throne and the elders. Though he had been slain, he is now standing and lives – an clear allusion to Jesus' resurrection from the dead.
- **The Lamb has seven horns**. In the Old Testament horns signify power, probably from the demonstration of might when two horned rams would fight (Deuteronomy 33:17). Seven is a number that often expresses the idea of completeness or perfection, so seven horns indicates complete might and strength. This is reflected in the Gospels by the

---

and the lamb overcame them, and destroyed them and trod them underfoot. And because of him the angels and men rejoiced, and all the land ... His kingdom is an everlasting kingdom, which shall not pass away." In this text, probably dated in the first century BC, the lion is a Messiah from Judah, while the lamb is a Messiah from Aaron. The lion and lamb in this passage are not contrasting figures, but variant symbols of one idea, the all prevailing Messiah. Beasley-Murray, *Revelation*, pp. 124-125.

risen Christ declaring, "All authority in heaven and on earth has been given to me" (Matthew 28:18).

- **The Lamb has seven eyes** – a bit grotesque if you take this literally. But seven eyes indicate that the Lamb sees fully, completely. The slain Lamb that stands is all powerful and all knowing – omnipotent and omniscient.

One of my favorite artistic illustrations of this scene of the Lamb standing in the throne room of heaven is a woodcut by Albrecht Dürer, "Adoration of the Lamb." His literal image of the slain lamb with seven horns and seven eyes appears a bit bizarre, but it is Dürer's direct way of conveying the same symbolism to those who view his work. A victorious Lamb

Detail of "Adoration of the Lamb" (1496-98) woodcut by Albrecht Dürer.

bearing a flag with a cross is known in Christian symbolism as the *Agnus Dei*, Latin for "the Lamb of God." Surrounding the Lamb are crowds of worshippers bearing palm branches.

Q2. (Revelation 5:6) Decode (that is, identify) each of the following symbols that relate to the Lamb:

The lamb itself represents ....

Standing after being slain indicates ...

Horns represent ....

Eyes represent ...

The number seven carries the idea of ...

To summarize, then, the Lamb has the qualities of being of ....
http://www.joyfulheart.com/forums/index.php?showtopic=72

Worshiping the Lamb Who Is Worthy (5:7-8)

Worship is due this Lamb. Falling prostrate before a king or deity is worship, humbling oneself before One who is greater.

> "The four living creatures and the twenty-four elders fell down before the Lamb. Each one had a harp and they were holding golden bowls full of incense, which are the prayers of the saints." (Revelation 5:8)

Sometimes I hear people make fun of harps, white robes, and clouds on which to sit and dangle one's feet. But if you consider the harp a kind of guitar with the elders singing praise choruses to the Lamb, maybe you can relate better to this scene. The 24 elders hold in their hands 24 golden bowls[6] filled with the prayers of God's people, symbolized as incense rising in a sweet smell before the throne as it is burned.

You and I may not be there in this heavenly enthronement ceremony, but our prayers are, valued with golden bowls that bear our petitions before the Lord. Our prayers are not forgotten, but heard in the very presence of the Almighty God on high!

God's people are referred to as "saints." The Greek adjective *hagios* bears the root meaning "pertaining to being dedicated or consecrated to the service of God, dedicated to God, holy, sacred, that is, reserved for God and God's service." Referring to people, it means, "the holy ones, believers, loyal followers, saints," speaking of Christians as consecrated to God.[7] We are not called saints because we are perfect, but because we have been made holy by Christ, sanctified, set apart for God's own service and use. You and I are these holy ones, dedicated to God himself.

A Song of Redemption (5:9-10)

The song the elders sing is a "new song," one not heard before. It is sung upon the occasion of enthroning the triumphant, conquering Lamb. Examine the words with me, for the song explains the basis of the Lamb's worthiness to open the scroll and execute its kingdom, its promises, and the awesome events leading up to the end.

> "And they sang a new song:
> 'You are worthy to take the scroll
> and to open its seals,
> because (*hoti*) you were slain
> and with your blood you purchased (*agorazō*) men for God
> from every tribe and language and people and nation.
> You have made them to be a kingdom and priests

---

[6] "Bowls" is the Greek noun *phialē* which refers specifically to a bowl used in offerings (BDAG 1055).

[7] *Hagios*, BDAG 10-11.

> to serve our God,
> and they will reign on the earth.'" (Revelation 5:9-10)

The song explains the Lamb's worthiness with a clause beginning with the Greek conjunction *hoti*, used here as a "marker of causality, subordinating, because, since."[8] The Lamb is able to execute God's plan for the Last Days because he was slain and with the blood produced by his own sacrificial death, presumably, he "purchased men for God."

"Purchased" (NIV), "ransomed" (NRSV), and "redeemed" (KJV) translate the Greek verb *agorazō*. In terms of things, it means "to acquire things or services in exchange for money, buy, purchase." With regards to persons it means "to secure the rights to someone by paying a price, buy, acquire as property."[9]

Notice that John the Revelator does not provide a theory of the atonement, *per se*, but states matter-of-factly, that by the Lamb's blood he redeemed enslaved men and now owns them as his servants, his saints, his set-apart people. How? We're not told. Why? He doesn't say at this point. But for this victorious feat, the Lamb is worshipped and praised.

And what of the redeemed? Who are they? Not just God's chosen people, the Jews, but now from every tribe, language, people, and nation (*ethnē*) – throngs of people from around the globe are purchased for God.

---

[8] *Hoti*, BDAG 731-732.
[9] *Agorazō*, BDAG 14. See also Morris, *Apostolic Preaching*, pp. 50-52.

> Q3. (Revelation 5:5) What has the Lamb done to "triumph" and so become worthy to take the scroll and open its seals? (Hint: See the "for" or "because" clause in 5:9 for the answer.)
> http://www.joyfulheart.com/forums/index.php?showtopic=73

A Song of Praise (5:11-12)

Now the millions of angels sing a second song in praise to the Lamb:

> "Worthy is the Lamb, who was slain,
> to receive power and wealth and wisdom and strength
> and honor and glory and praise!" (Revelation 5:12)

They sing, not just to the Lamb, but to "the Lamb who was slain." Not only is he worthy to open the scroll and break its seals, he is also worthy of praise in his own right. When you add up the number of elements of praise found in this song of praise, and you'll grasp the truth conveyed here, that the Lamb is worthy of *all* praise – seven-fold perfect, fulfilled, complete praise!

A Song to the Divine Lamb (5:13-14)

The third song of praise is not sung by just the 24 elders or millions of angels. This song is sung by every creature or created thing (human, animal, vegetable, mineral?) in both heaven and earth, the underworld and the mysterious deep.

> "Then I heard every creature in heaven and on earth and under
> the earth and on the sea, and all that is in them, singing:
>
> 'To him who sits on the throne and to the Lamb
> be praise and honor and glory and power,
> for ever and ever!'

> The four living creatures said, 'Amen,' and the elders fell down
> and worshiped." (Revelation 5:13-14)

Notice that this worship is directed toward both "him who sits on the throne," that is, God the Father (in Trinitarian terminology), but also to the Lamb.

"Worshipped" in verse 14 is the Greek verb *proskuneō*, "to express in attitude or gesture one's complete dependence on or submission to a high authority figure, (fall down and) worship, do obeisance to, prostrate oneself before, do reverence to...."[10]

Isn't it sacrilege for a creature to receive praise along with God? Yes. But the Lamb is no creature. He is God – God the Son. As Paul writes:

> **"Who, being in very nature God**...
> he humbled himself
> and became obedient to death –
> even death on a cross!
> Therefore God exalted him to the highest place
> and gave him the name that is above every name,
> that **at the name of Jesus every knee should bow,**
> **in heaven and on earth and under the earth,**
> **and every tongue confess that Jesus Christ is Lord,**
> **to the glory of God the Father."** (Philippians 2:6, 8b-11)

Now God *has* highly exalted him. Every knee is bowing and every tongue – "every creature in heaven and on earth and under the earth and on the sea" – is confessing that Jesus Christ is Lord. And God the Father receives glory from it, too, since the Father and the Son are One. Notice that these songs of praise in Revelation 5 teach us that not only God the Father, but Jesus the Son, is also to be worshipped and praised.

---

[10] *Proskuneō*, BDAG 882-883.

Q4. (5:13-14) What does it tell us about the status of the Lamb that he is worshipped alongside "him who sits on the throne"? http://www.joyfulheart.com/forums/index.php?showtopic=75

Jesus, "the Lamb of God, who takes away the sin of the world" – and your sin as well as mine – this Jesus is worthy of our worship and praise. In Revelation 5, heaven can't seem to restrain itself. It breaks out in songs of praises to the Lamb again and again. As we come to know and appreciate Jesus the Lamb of God, we too will desire to praise him more and more.

This coming Easter, join your voices with multitudes who sing the great song of praise:

"Crown him with many crowns, the Lamb upon his throne,
Hark! how the heavenly anthem drowns all music but its own.
Awake, my soul, and sing of him who died for thee,
and hail him as thy matchless King through all eternity.

"Crown him the Lord of love! behold his hands and side,
those wounds, yet visible above, in beauty glorified...."

Concluding:

"All hail, Redeemer, hail! For thou hast died for me;
thy praise shall never, never fail throughout eternity."[11]

Behold, the Lamb of God, who takes away the sin of the world!

---

[11] "Crown Him with Many Crowns," words by Matthew Bridges (1800-1894), an Anglican and later Roman Catholic, and Godfrey Thring (1823-1903) who added the final stanza, "Crown him the Lord of Life...."

Prayer

Oh, Lamb of God, we do worship you with other saints of God around the world. You have redeemed us by your death and resurrection, and now we are yours. Not unwilling slaves, but servants out of love and respect and honor and everlasting gratitude. We love you, Lord Jesus, and lift up your name as Holy! Holy! Holy! Amen. Hallelujah!

Key Verses

"You are worthy to take the scroll
and to open its seals,
because you were slain,
and with your blood you purchased men for God
from every tribe and language and people and nation.
You have made them to be
a kingdom and priests to serve our God,
and they will reign on the earth." (Revelation 5:9-10)

Appendix 1. Theories of the Atonement

Anchor and fish, tomb slab from Catacomb of Domitilla, Rome, 3rd century A.D. A combination of a cross and an anchor, emblematic of faith and hope. It was often used as a sacred symbol in the catacombs.

How can sinful man ever be accepted by a holy God? Many theories have been put forward to try to explain what is said in the scripture. All seem to have some aspect of the vast, complex truth of the atonement.[1] Theories generally follow one of two directions:

1. **Subjective.** The effect of the cross on the sinner.
2. **Objective.** What the atonement achieves quite outside the individual.

---

[1] The English word "atone" means "to supply satisfaction for, expiate," and derives from Middle English *at* + *one*, "to become reconciled." (*Merriam Webster's Collegiate Dictionary*, 10th Edition.)

These are over simplifications of the various theories, but enough to give you the gist of the argument.

1. **Moral Influence Theory**. Describes the subjective effects of Christ's cross on the sinner. Abelard teaches that when we look at the cross we see the greatness of divine love, which delivers us from fear and produces in us an answering love, putting aside selfishness and sin. Popular among scholars in the liberal school.
2. **Atonement as Victory**. Sees sinful people as belonging to Satan. God offers his Son to Satan as a ransom, but Christ cannot be held in hell and rises the third day in victory. Popular with the early church fathers.
3. **Anselm's Satisfaction Theory**. Sin dishonors the majesty of a sovereign God. To offer appropriate satisfaction to the offense would require one as great as God himself, but must be offered by a one who is man. Thus the God-man is needed to provide full satisfaction for sin.
4. **Penal Substitution**. The wages of man's sin is death. Christ endures death and God's punishment for sin in our stead. Popular with the Reformers.
5. **Sacrifice**. Christ's saving act is a sacrifice for sin.
6. **Governmental Theory**. Grotius argues that Christ did not bear our punishment, but suffered as a penal example whereby the law is honored while sinners are pardoned.[2]

Which of these is true? All have elements of truth in them but some are inadequate to stand alone. A better question may be: Which are clearly supported in the Bible? I'm not trying to

[2] Leon Morris, "Atonement, Theories of the," in Walter A. Elwell (ed.), *Evangelical Dictionary of Theology* (Baker, 1984), pp. 100-102. Geoffrey W. Bromiley, "Atone," *International Standard Biblical Encyclopedia* 1:352-360. C.M. Tuckett, "Atonement in the NT," *Anchor Bible Dictionary* 1:518-522. Wayne Grudem, *Systematic Theology* (Zondervan, 1994, 2000), pp. 579-582, 586.

promote a particular theory but stimulate you to thoughtfully examine what the Bible actually teaches.

Appendix 2. Classic Protestant Liberalism and the Atonement: A Plea for Reconsideration

As I've studied what the Bible says about Christ's atonement for our sins, I've become increasingly aware of Classic Protestant Liberalism's intolerance of any view of Jesus' death being a blood sacrifice for the atonement of our sins. Why is that? I wonder.

Characteristics of Classic Protestant Liberalism

Let's examine some characteristics of Liberal Christianity that came out of the Enlightenment. (Note: I'm not using the term "liberal" in the careless way that Rush Limbaugh might, but as a technical term to describe a certain approach to Christianity.)[1]

Salvador Dali, "Crucifixion (Corpus Hypercubus)" (1954), Oil on canvas, 194.5 x 124 cm. Metropolitan Museum of Art, New York.

1. Exalts life and action over "constricting dogma," doctrine, and thought.
2. Tends to focus on human experience and reason (anthropocentric) rather than divine revelation (theocentric).

[1] As outlined in M. Eugene Boring, *Disciples and the Bible* (Chalice Press, 1997), pp. 215-216.

3. Sees God's presence to be immanent in the world, working through human experience.
4. Holds Jesus to be a model to pattern one's life after, rather than the one through whom God acted to save mankind – "The religion *of* Jesus rather than the religion *about* Jesus."
5. Looks at salvation as this worldly and social rather than eschatological.
6. Views the Bible as a record of humanity's search for and experience of God, rather than a vehicle for the transcendent word of God.

Some of these approaches to Christianity may be fruitful. For example, the stress on justice for the oppressed must be recovered for our churches to be balanced.

A Liberal Approach to the Atonement

Here is the route many Classic Protestant Liberals take with the doctrine of the Atonement. I'm over-simplifying a bit, but not very much:

1. The New Testament is rich with explanations of Jesus' death on the cross as a substitutionary sacrifice for our sins.
2. The background of sacrifice is the Old Testament system of animal sacrifices to atone for sin.
3. But animal sacrifice is a primitive concept found in most ancient religions to appease the wrath of an angry god. From a comparative religions standpoint, some scholars presume that animal sacrifices in Israel are no different.
4. Such a view of a substitutionary atonement depicts a violent, angry, bloodthirsty god that seems antithetical to the God of whom Jesus speaks, who is loving and forgiving.

5. Therefore, the Old Testament view of appeasing an angry God is unacceptable to Christians. Therefore, we reject it and any view of substitutionary atonement.
6. Moreover, punishing one person for the sins of others offends our sense of fairness.
7. Rather than think about Jesus' crucifixion as an event that changes God's relationship to us by atoning for sin (objective theory of the atonement), it is viewed an event that helps us see Jesus' love and commitment toward us that melts our hearts and changes us into loving people, too (subjective theory of the atonement).[2]

Many people with this view are sincere, moral people who are trying to deal with a discrepancy that they see in Scripture. They stress a progressive revelation with the New Testament at the apex and Love being the key to it all.

A Dishonest and Demeaning Caricature

However, the God revealed in the Old Testament *is* the same as the God that Jesus told us about. Consider the classic self-revelation of God to Moses:

> "The LORD, the LORD, the compassionate and gracious God, slow to anger, abounding in love and faithfulness, maintaining love to thousands, and forgiving wickedness, rebellion and sin. Yet he does not leave the guilty unpunished...." (Exodus 34:6-7)

To describe the God of the Old Testament as an angry, blood-thirsty god is a demeaning caricature, a flimsy straw man, and reflects a dishonest handling of Scripture. Yes, the biblical God shows anger against sin – both in the Old Testament and the New. So do moral people everywhere.

---

[2] The subjective theory of the atonement contains a profound truth, but is inadequate by itself to explain the teaching of the New Testament which requires some kind of a substitutionary atonement.

The Downside of Classic Liberalism

Classic Liberalism, for all its positive aspects, contains seeds that can seriously distort Christianity. In some of its forms, at least:

1. **Classic Protestant Liberalism can make human reason the authority rather than Biblical revelation.** Where reason and the teaching of Scripture conflict, the Scripture tends to be rejected. When we give the human mind a greater authority than the Bible, we are no longer open to being corrected by any teaching we disagree with. This reduces what we can learn from God to what we can wrap our minds around – and thus severely reduces the size of the God we can accept. How big is your God? As big as the God Jesus and the Apostles believed in?

2. **Classic Protestant Liberalism can render Bible interpretation dependent upon theological fads.** Classic Protestant Liberals sometimes justify their position by scholarly questioning of the authority or authenticity of Bible passages they find theologically distasteful. But theological and biblical scholarship is notoriously faddish. Yesterday's theory is reduced within a decade or two to a footnote obituary in the Next Great Theology. Rather than rely on transient scholarly trends, wise Christians base their faith on the Scripture passages that speak clearly, and interpret the obscure passages in light of the clear ones,

3. **Classic Protestant Liberalism can reduce preaching to parroting the wisdom of popular writers,** parenting gurus, and pop-psychology, with the veneer of a scripture text as a jumping off place. Instead of seeking to understand what the Bible actually says and teaching that to the congregation, some preachers find it easier to provide their own wisdom and answers to life's questions.

4. **Classic Protestant Liberalism can produce congregations of biblically illiterate members** who have acquired an immunity to any serious teaching from the Bible.

The Jesus Seminar Fallacy

Let me give you an example. As I was working on this Bible study, I spoke to a Classic Protestant Liberal professor who had taught New Testament at the college level. I asked, "About the Words of Institution in Matthew, 'This is my blood of the covenant which is poured out for many for the forgiveness of sins,' certainly sound like the language of sacrifice that Jesus uses as an explanation for his death. How do *you* understand it?"

"Well," he responded kindly, "we don't really know if Jesus uttered those actual words." Then he went on to tell me about a non-violent theory of the atonement that doesn't rely on the idea of blood sacrifice.

This approach reminds me of reductionism of the Jesus Seminar variety that questions 80% of Jesus' sayings as inauthentic. What some scholars don't like theologically, they can excuse as possibly inauthentic. Convenient. When you examine the sort of form and source critical scholarship that decisions of the Jesus Seminar were based on, you can see how seriously speculation and theory have undermined the authority of Jesus himself.[3]

Revulsion at Animal Sacrifice

My dear friends, when we study about animal sacrifice in the Old Testament we *ought* to be revolted by the concept.

*   Not just because we are squeamish about slaughter since we are a generation or two removed from butchering animals on the farm – something our forebears have done for hundreds of years.

[3] For more on this see Ben Witherington III, H*The Jesus Quest: The Third Search for the Jew of Nazareth*H (Second Edition, InterVarsity Press, 1997), chapter 2.

- Not because we are PETA adherents who believe that an animal has a soul every bit as valuable as a human's.[4]

But because animal sacrifice reveals how offensive and repugnant our sins are to a holy God. Animal sacrifice taught the Old Testament believers that they could not come into the presence of this holy God without their sins being cleansed. The people of the Old Testament were originally herdsmen and for them animals functioned as currency. Animal sacrifice taught them that the cost of atonement is very, very high. How astronomically high, they didn't have a clue!

A Plea for Reconsideration

This is my plea to pastors and teachers in denominations where Classic Protestant Liberalism has a strong hold. If you reject the concept of Jesus' death as a sacrifice for sin, that's your right as a free person, but I plead with you to maintain intellectual and moral integrity with the text of Scripture. You flock needs you to tell them what the Scripture actually teaches, not your theological reservations and doubts. Please don't, for the sake of keeping your job, nurture private redefinitions of biblical words so that you can pretend you believe the Bible. My dear friend, much is at stake here, for it is indisputable that:

- The New Testament teaches Jesus' sacrifice for our sins as the Lamb of God. This is not just one theory of the atonement from which to pick and choose. The New Testament *very obviously* teaches this. I'll document this for several scripture texts in the Lamb of God Bible Study.
- The Words of Institution in Matthew clearly state: "This is my blood of the covenant which is poured out for many for the forgiveness of sins." This is the language of sacrifice. It is only fair to acknowledge that the Church, from

---

[4] PETA stands for People for the Ethical Treatment of Animals.

the very earliest times down to our own, has commemo-
rated in the Eucharist the sacrificial death of Jesus for our
sins.

- The very basic credo of the early church specifically af-
firms "that Christ died for our sins according to the Scripture" (1 Corinthians 15:3).

The concept of the substitutionary atonement is not some far
right fundamentalist doctrine. It is at the core of a New Testament
faith and has been taught by the respected Fathers and Reformers
of the Church century after century.

I'm not trying to pretend that I understand all the nuances of a
perfect theory of the atonement as presented in the Bible. I have
some unanswered questions, some points I'd like clarified further.
But I do know this. The New Testament clearly teaches some form
of a substitutionary atonement.

Yes, you can reject a substitutionary atonement by Jesus. And
there'll be many colleagues who'll support you. You won't be
alone in your opinion. But I'm just naive enough to appeal to you
to rethink your position in light of the New Testament's teaching.

My dear brothers and sisters in Christ, the teaching of Jesus
and the Apostles that has come down to us in Scripture *is worthy*
of our belief and allegiance, even if we can't comprehend it fully.
We can come again to the plain text of Scripture itself, uncolored
by what unbelievers and skeptics of this age might say, and find
afresh what God has done for us through Jesus Christ. Let us
allow God speak to us through the Scriptures that we might be
renewed in the spirit of our minds.

Appendix 3. Quotations, References and Allusions in the New Testament to Isaiah 53 and other Servant Songs

Some of these allusions are very clear. Others use parallel concepts that probably have their root in Isaiah 53. Where appropriate, I have boldfaced the words that are central to the allusion or parallel. Verses are listed in the order they appear in the New Testament. The left column shows the corresponding verse in Isaiah.

42:1   And a voice came from heaven: "You are my Son, whom I love; with you I am well pleased." Mark 1:11 = Matthew 3:17

42:1-4   "Here is **my servant** whom I have chosen,
the one I love, in whom I delight;
I will put my Spirit on him,
and he will proclaim justice to the nations.
He will not quarrel or cry out;
no one will hear his voice in the streets.
A bruised reed he will not break,
and a smoldering wick he will not snuff out,
till he leads justice to victory.
In his name the nations will put their hope." (Matthew 12:18-21; quotes Is 42:1-4)

52:12-   "just as the Son of Man did not come to be served, but **to**
53:12   **serve**, and to give his life as a **ransom for many**." (Matthew 20:28=Mark 10:45; conceptual parallel. See "for many" language in Is 53:11-12)

53:11-   "This is my blood of the covenant, which is poured out

12	**for many** for the forgiveness of sins." (Matthew 26:28 = Mark 14:24)
53:3	"Jesus replied, 'To be sure, Elijah does come first, and restores all things. Why then is it written that the Son of Man must **suffer** much and **be rejected**?'"(Mark 9:12)
53:4	"This was to fulfill what was spoken through the prophet Isaiah: **'He took up our infirmities and carried our diseases.'**" (Matthew 8:17; quotes Is 53:4)
53:12	"It is written: **'And he was numbered with the transgressors'**; and I tell you that this must be fulfilled in me. Yes, what is written about me is reaching its fulfillment." (Luke 22:37; Jesus quotes Is 53:12)
53:1-12, 52:13	"He said to them, 'How foolish you are, and how slow of heart to believe all that the prophets have spoken! Did not the Christ **have to suffer these things and then enter his glory?**' And beginning with Moses and all the Prophets, he explained to them what was said in all the Scriptures concerning himself." (Luke 24:25-27)
53:6-7, 12	"The next day John saw Jesus coming toward him and said, 'Look, the **Lamb** of God, who **takes away the sin of the world!**'" (John 1:29)
	"When he saw Jesus passing by, he said, 'Look, the **Lamb of God!**' " (John 1:36)
52:13	"The crowd spoke up, 'We have heard from the Law that the Christ will remain forever, so how can you say, "The Son of Man must **be lifted up**"? Who is this "Son of Man"?'" (John 12:34)
53:1	"This was to fulfill the word of Isaiah the prophet: 'LORD, who has believed our message and to whom has

the arm of the LORD been revealed?'" (John 12:38, quotes Is 53:1)

53:7-8   "The eunuch was reading this passage of Scripture:
          'He was led like a sheep to the slaughter
          and as a lamb before the shearer is silent,
          so he did not open his mouth.
          In his humiliation he was deprived of justice.
          Who can speak of his descendants?
          For his life was taken from the earth.'
          The eunuch asked Philip, 'Tell me, please, who is the
          prophet talking about, himself or someone else?' Then
          Philip began with that very passage of Scripture and told
          him the good news about Jesus." (Acts 8:32-35; quotes Is
          53:7-8)

53:11-   "Again, the gift of God is not like the result of the one
12   man's sin: The judgment followed one sin and brought
          condemnation, but the gift followed **many trespasses**
          and brought **justification**." (Romans 5:16)

          "For just as through the disobedience of the one man **the
          many** were made sinners, so also through the obedience
          of the one man **the many will be made righteous**."
          (Romans 5:19)

53:1   "But not all the Israelites accepted the good news. For
          Isaiah says, **'Lord, who has believed our message?'**"
          (Romans 10:16, quotes Is 53:1)

52:15   "Rather, as it is written:
          'Those who were not told about him will see,
          and those who have not heard will understand.'"
          (Romans 15:21, quotes Is 52:15)

53.1-12   "For what I received I passed on to you as of first importance: that Christ **died for our sins according to the Scriptures**, that he was buried, that he was raised on the third day according to the Scriptures, and that he appeared to Peter, and then to the Twelve." (1 Cor. 15:3-5)

53:11   "God **made him who had no sin to be sin for us**, so that in him we might **become the righteousness** of God." (2 Cor. 5:21, conceptual parallel)

53:6, 12   "Who **gave himself for our sins** to rescue us from the present evil age, according to the will of our God and Father." (Galatians 1:4)

"I have been crucified with Christ and I no longer live, but Christ lives in me. The life I live in the body, I live by faith in the Son of God, who loved me and **gave himself for me**." (Galatians 2:20)

"...and live a life of love, just as Christ loved us and **gave himself up for us** as a fragrant offering and sacrifice to God." (Ephesians 5:2)

"Husbands, love your wives, just as Christ loved the church and **gave himself up for her**." (Ephesians 5:25)

53:10   "For there is one God and one mediator between God and men, the man Christ Jesus, who **gave himself as a ransom** for all men – the testimony given in its proper time." (1 Tim. 2:5-6)

53:10   "Who **gave himself for us to redeem us** from all wickedness and to purify for himself a people that are his very own, eager to do what is good." (Titus 2:14)

53:4, 6,   "so Christ was sacrificed once **to take away the sins** of
11, 12   many people; and he will appear a second time, not **to bear sin**, but to bring salvation to those who are waiting

for him." (Hebrews 9:28)

52:13-   "...Trying to find out the time and circumstances to
53:12   which the Spirit of Christ in them was pointing when he
         predicted the sufferings of Christ and the glories that
         would follow." (1 Peter 1:11)

53:11, 9, "To this you were called, because **Christ suffered for
7, 5, 6   you**, leaving you an example, that you should follow in
           his steps.

> "He committed no sin,
> and no deceit was found in his mouth." (quotes Is
> 53:9)

When they hurled their insults at him, he did not
retaliate; when he suffered, he made no threats. Instead,
he entrusted himself to him who judges justly. He
himself **bore our sins** in his body on the tree, so that we
might die to sins and live for righteousness; **by his
wounds you have been healed.** (quotes Is 53:5) For you
were **like sheep going astray**, but now you have
returned to the Shepherd and Overseer of your souls." (1
Peter 2:24-25)

53:11   "For Christ **died for sins** once for all, the **righteous for
         the unrighteous**, to bring you to God. He was put to
         death in the body but made alive by the Spirit..." (1 Peter
         3:18)

53:11   "He is the **atoning sacrifice for our sins**, and not only
         for ours but also for the **sins of the whole world**." (1
         John 2:2)

5:4, 6,   "But you know that he appeared so that he might **take
11, 12   away our sins**. And in him is no sin." (1 John 3:5)

53:10   "This is love: not that we loved God, but that he loved us

and sent his Son as an **atoning sacrifice for our sins**." (1
John 4:10)

Appendix 4. Boys' Philosophies, C.S. Lewis

An excerpt from C.S. Lewis, *Mere Christianity* (Macmillan, 1952), Book 2, Chapter 2, "The Invasion":

C.S. Lewis
(1898-1963)

Atheism is too simple. And I will tell you another view that is also too simple. It is the view I call Christianity-and-water, the view which simply says there is a good God in Heaven and everything is all right – leaving out all the difficult and terrible doctrines about sin and hell and the devil, and the redemption. Both these are boys' philosophies.

It is no good asking for a simple religion. After all, real things are not simple. They look simple, but they are not. The table I am sitting at looks simple: but ask a scientist to tell you what it is really made of–all about the atoms and how the light waves rebound from them and hit my eye and what they do to the optic nerve and what it does to my brain–and, of course, you find that what we call 'seeing a table' lands you in mysteries and complications which you can hardly get to the end of.

A child saying a child's prayer looks simple. And if you are content to stop there, well and good. But if you are not and the modern world usually is not – if you want to go on and ask what is really happening – then you must be prepared for something difficult. If we ask for something more than simplicity, it is silly then to complain that the something more is not simple.

Very often, however, this silly procedure is adopted by people who are not silly, but who, consciously or unconsciously, want to destroy Christianity. Such people put up a version of Christianity suitable for a child of six and make that the object of their attack.

When you try to explain the Christian doctrine as it is really held by an instructed adult, they then complain that you are making their heads turn round and that it is all too complicated and that if there really were a God they are sure He would have made 'religion' simple, because simplicity is so beautiful, etc. You must be on your guard against these people for they will change their ground every minute and only waste your time. Notice, too, their idea of God 'making religion simple'; as if 'religion' were something God invented, and not His statement to us of certain quite unalterable facts about His own nature.

Besides being complicated, reality, in my experience, is usually odd. It is not neat, not obvious, not what you expect....

Appendix 5: Participant Notes

Please feel free to duplicate these discussion questions for any group that you are leading at no extra charge. They are also available free online in 8-1/2 x 11" format for reproduction for your class at:

www.jesuswalk.com/lamb/lamb_lesson_handouts.pdf

These notes consist of some of the key definitions of words, an overall outline of the lesson and the discussion questions for your group to talk about. In some cases I've left some blanks to be filled in, with answers at the end of that week's notes.

You may use these notes for a class which you teach. They are specifically designed to be used for classes conducted using the Lamb of God DVD at a modest price from

www.jesuswalk.com/books/lamb.htm

The DVD includes the following lessons:

		Length
1.	**Behold the Lamb and basic concepts of sacrifice** (John 1:29).	22:03
2.	**The Lamb Who Takes Our Place** (Isaiah 53)	24:32
3.	**The Lamb that Redeems Us from Slavery** (1 Peter 1:18-19)	22:10
4.	**The Passover Lamb of Whom We Partake** (Exodus 12)	20:32
5.	**The Triumphant Lamb We Worship** (Revelation 5)	22:00

A 45-second Promotional Clip is also included which can be used to promote your class in church, if your church has the ability to project from a DVD.

I have also prepared audio recordings for each lesson. The follow pretty closely the lessons in this book, though are slightly different lengths than shown above. They don't include Appendices 1-4. They are not available for sale, but are online in MP3 format and may be downloaded from

http://www.jesuswalk.com/lamb/lamb.htm

Feel free to use them for personal use or to play in your group if you have the ability to play MP3 format recordings. They also indicate pauses for each discussion question.

May God richly bless you as you teach about Jesus' atonement using these materials.

1. Behold, the Lamb of God – Basic Concepts of Sacrifice (John 1:29)

John the Baptist's Prophetic Insight (John 1:29)

airō, "to lift up and move from one place to another," here "to take away, remove blot out."

Q1. (John 1:29) How do you know that John the Baptist's statement about the Lamb of God refers to sacrifice? How was the comprehensiveness of "sin of the world" so radical a concept?

Ancient Animal Sacrifice

Holiness, Anger, and Justice

"The LORD, the LORD, the compassionate and gracious God, slow to anger, abounding in love and faithfulness, maintaining love to thousands, and forgiving wickedness, rebellion and sin. Yet he does not leave the guilty unpunished." (Exodus 34:6-7)

Q2. Why is anger an appropriate response to sin? What is the difference between capricious or uncontrolled anger and anger that brings about justice?

Q3. Why is animal sacrifice repulsive to modern people? How much of this has to do with a city vs. a farming way of life?

Atonement

"For the life of a creature is in the blood, and I have given it to you to make atonement for yourselves on the altar; it is the blood that makes atonement for one's life." (Leviticus 17:11)

kāpar, kipper, "to make an atonement, make reconciliation, purge ... to wipe clean, purge."

Middle English "at-one-ment" or "reconciliation."

Basic Elements of Sacrifice for Sin (Leviticus 5:5-6; 4:32-35)

1. _____ of the sin
2. **Bringing an animal** that has **no** _____
3. **Lay his** _____ on its head (4:33a; Leviticus 16:21)
4. _____ **the animal** by cutting its throat (4:33b)
5. _____ **is collected** by a priest, put on the horns of the altar, and poured out at the base of the altar (4:34)
6. _____ **portions burned on the altar** (4:35).
7. **Meat is** _____.

Principles of Sacrifice

1. _____ or acknowledgement of sin is a necessary part of the sacrifice.
2. A sacrificial animal is _____ to the sinner.
3. There is a _____ between the sinner and the sacrifice.
4. Killing the animal is very _____

Q4. (Leviticus 4:32-35; 5:5-6) What are the basic elements involved in a sacrifice for sin? Which of these are still necessary for forgiveness of sins today? Which are no longer necessary? Why?

Forgiveness and Grace of God

"It is impossible for the blood of bulls and goats to take away sins" (Hebrews 10:4)

Q5. In what sense is God's provision of animal sacrifice for forgiveness of sins an expression of his mercy? Were animal sacrifices actually adequate to atone for human sin?

Q6. What do you think God intended animal sacrifice teach us about sin? What do they teach us about holiness? What do they teach us about God's nature?

Answers to blanks: confession, defect, hands, slay, blood, fat, eaten. confession, costly, close identification, personal

2. The Lamb Who Took Our Place (Isaiah 53)

Read Isaiah 52:13 - 53:12

Universal Atonement

Servant Songs, Servant of Yahweh, Suffering Servant (Isaiah 40-55)

Scope of the Servant's ministry: " *many nations*" (52:15), "*all.*" (53:6), " *my people*" (53:8), " *many*" (53:11), "*many*" (53:12).

Q1. From how large a group of people does God remove sins in Isaiah 52:13 - 53:12? In what sense is this a universal sacrifice of salvation? In what sense is Jesus' sacrifice wasted on some people?

Jesus Saw His Ministry as a Fulfillment of Isaiah 53

"...Just as the Son of Man did not come to be served, but to serve, and to give his life as a ransom for many." (Mark 10:45)

Parallel ideas: (1) the servanthood, (2) atoning death, (3) the idea of voluntarily giving one's life, and (4) the wording "for many," which parallels the words "many" (53:11) and "of many" (53:12).

"This is my blood of the covenant, which is poured out for many for the forgiveness of sins." (Matthew 26:28)

"Why then is it written that the Son of Man must suffer much and be rejected?"(Mark 9:12)

"'Did not the Christ have to suffer these things and then enter his glory?" (Luke 24:25-27)

"It is written: 'And he was numbered with the transgressors'; and I tell you that this must be fulfilled in me. Yes, what is written about me is reaching its fulfillment." (Luke 22:37)

Q2. Which New Testament parallels to Isaiah 53 convince you that Jesus himself saw his own mission and destiny spelled out in Isaiah 53? If you aren't convinced, what stands in your way?

Isaiah 53 is a complex passage. My approach won't be a verse-by-verse commentary, but a topical study of five themes which relate to Jesus' work of atonement.

1. The Servant Is a Substitute Who Bears Our _____

"Our infirmities ... our sorrows..." (53:4), "our transgressions ... our iniquities..." (53:5), "... the iniquity of us all," (53:6), "... a guilt offering..." (53:10), "... their iniquities" (53:11), " sin of many" (53:12).

- *'āshem*, which means "offering for sin, sin, trespass offering."
- *nāśā'* – "lift, carry, take... of bearing the guilt or punishment of sin... the taking away, forgiveness, or pardon of sin, iniquity, and transgression."
- *sābal* – "bear, transport (such as a heavy load)."
- *pâga'* – "to lay, burden"

"God made him who had no sin to be sin for us, so that in him we might become the righteousness of God." (2 Corinthians 5:21)

"To this you were called, because Christ suffered for you, leaving you an example, that you should follow in his steps. 'He committed no sin, and no deceit was found in his mouth.' When they hurled their insults at him, he did not retaliate; when he suffered, he made no threats. Instead, he entrusted himself to him who judges justly. He himself bore our sins in his body on the tree, so that we might die to sins and live for righteousness; 'by his wounds you have been healed.' For you were like sheep going astray, but now you have returned to the Shepherd and Overseer of your souls." (1 Peter 2:24-25)

2. The Servant Is a Substitute Who Bears Our _____

"Stricken ...smitten ... afflicted" (53:4), "oppressed and afflicted..." (53:7), "crush ... cause him to suffer ..." (53:10).

"But he was *pierced* for our transgressions, he was *crushed* for our iniquities; the *punishment* that brought us peace was *upon him*, and by his wounds we are healed." (53:5)

"For the transgression of my people he was *stricken*." (53:8)

Federal headship

> Q3. Isaiah 53 teaches what theologians call "the substitutionary atonement." In what sense does the Servant act as a substitute to bear our *sins*? Put it in your own words.

> Q4. In addition to our *sins*, the Servant also bears the *punishment* deserved by sinners. In what sense, if any, did Jesus bear the punishment due you when he died on the cross?

3. The Servant Acts _____

"He poured out...." (53:12), "took up ... carried..." (53:4), "he did not open his mouth" (53:7).

4. The Servant Acts as a _____

"... So will he sprinkle many nations" (52:15); "By his knowledge my righteous servant will justify many..." (53:11)

5. The Servant Is _____ by God

"Raised and lifted up and highly exalted." (52:13), "I will give him a portion among the great..." (53:12).

Philippians 2:9-11

"After the suffering of his soul, he will see the light of life and be satisfied..." (53:11, NIV)

Q5. Which single New Testament passage best sums up for you the lessons of Isaiah 53? Why did you chose this passage? Select from Matt. 26:38-42; Luke 22:37; John 1:29; Romans 3:24-26; 2 Corinthians 5:20-21; 1 Peter 2:24-25; 1 Peter 3:18; Philippians 2:5-11 – or any other passage you can think of.

Answers to blanks: sin, punishment, willingly, priest, exalted

3. The Lamb Who Redeems Us from Slavery (1 Pet 1:18-19)

"For you know that it was not with perishable things such as silver or gold that you were **redeemed** from the empty way of life handed down to you from your forefathers, but with the precious blood of Christ, a **lamb** without blemish or defect." (1 Peter 1:18-19)

Slavery in the Ancient World

Slavery came about through warfare, piracy, brigandage, the international slave trade, kidnapping, infant exposure, failure to pay a debt, forced labor of alien populations, natural reproduction of the existing slave population, and the punishment of criminals to the mines or gladiatorial combat.

> Q1. In the New Testament world, what class of humans was freed by payment of a redemption price or a ransom? Why do you think that Jesus, Peter, and Paul used this analogy in this week's theme verses. What aspect of the Christian life does it help explain?

The Old Testament Kinsman-Redeemer

"I am the LORD, and I will bring you out from under the yoke of the Egyptians. I will free you from being slaves to them, and I will redeem (*gā'al*) you with an outstretched arm and with mighty acts of judgment." (Exodus 6:6)

The Hebrew verb *gā'al* means "to redeem, avenge, revenge, ransom, and do the part of a kinsman:" (1) marrying a brother's widow if no children have yet been born, in order to raise up children in the brother's name, (2) purchasing family lands, (3) buying the freedom of relatives, (4) avenging a kinsman, (5) rescuing a kinsman.

pādâ, "ransom, rescue, deliver, to achieve the transfer of owner-ship from one to another through payment of a price or an equivalent substitute."

kōper, "ransom," from *kāpar*, which means "to atone by offering a substitute."

Q2. What comparisons do you see between Jesus and the role of the Old Testament type of the Kinsman-Redeemer?

Redeemed by the Lamb (1 Peter 1:18-19)

lytroō, "to free by paying a ransom, redeem."

"Without blemish or defect" (Exodus 12:5; 29:1; Leviticus 1:3, 10; 3:1, 6; 4:3, 23, 28, 32; etc.). Titus 2:12-14.

A Ransom for Many (Mark 10:44-45)

"For even the Son of Man did not come to be served, but to serve, and to give his life as a ransom (Greek *lytron*) for many." (Mark 10:44-45)

anti, "in place of, instead of."

Bought at a Price

"Do you not know that your body is a temple of the Holy Spirit, who is in you, whom you have received from God? You are not your own; you were bought at a price. Therefore honor God with your body." (1 Corinthians 6:19-20)

agorazō, "to secure the rights to someone by paying a price, buy, acquire as property."

1 Corinthians 7:23; Acts 20:28; 2 Peter 2:1l; Revelation 5:9; Revelation 14:4

Q3. (1 Corinthians 6:19-20) How should we disciples apply the principles: "You are not your own, you were bought with a price"? How should this affect our living?

Elements of the Slave Ransom Analogy

	1 Pet 1:18-19	**Mk 10:45**	**Acts 20:28**	**Rev 5:9**
Slaves	"you"	"for many"	church of God	people
Form of slavery	empty way of life	-	-	-
Ransom	Christ's blood	Jesus' life	"his own blood"	Lamb's blood
One to whom the ransom is paid	-	-	-	-
One who pays the ransom	unstated	Jesus	God	Lamb

Who or What Enslaves Us?

John 8:34; Galatians 4:9; Titus 3:3; Romans 6:17, 22; 7:21-25a)

Satan Is Defeated, Not Paid Off

Devil Ransom Theory

Mark 3:24-27; Acts 26:17-18; Luke 4:18-19; Colossians 1:13-14; cf.
John 10:10; Revelation 12:10-12
John 8:32; Col. 2:13-15; Romans 8:1-9

Q4. According to the slave-ransom analogy, who is the slave?
What is he enslaved by? Who offers the ransom? If Satan is
involved in the enslaving process, why isn't the ransom paid
to him? Why isn't the slave-ransom analogy spelled out
completely in the New Testament?

Q5. Extra Credit: In what sense have we been set free or
released from slavery to sin? Why do we need the Holy Spirit
to help us keep this freedom?

Atonement for Our Sins

4. The Passover Lamb of Whom We Partake (1 Cor 5:7)

"Get rid of the old yeast that you may be a new batch without yeast – as you really are. For Christ, our Passover lamb, has been sacrificed." (1 Corinthians 5:7)

The Plague on the Firstborn

"Then they are to take some of the blood and put it on the sides and tops of the doorframes of the houses where they eat the lambs." (Exodus 12:7)

"The blood will be a sign for you on the houses where you are; and when I see the blood, I will pass over you. No destructive plague will touch you when I strike Egypt." (Exodus 12:13)

"When the LORD goes through the land to strike down the Egyptians, he will see the blood on the top and sides of the doorframe and will pass over that doorway, and he will not permit the destroyer to enter your houses and strike you down." (Exodus 12:23)

pāsach, 1. "to pass (over)," the merciful passing over of a destructive power. 2. "to defend, protect."

The Sacrifice of the Passover Lamb

The lamb seems to be a kind of substitute or interposition for the firstborn males and animals in the household.

Q1. (Exodus 12) In what way did the lambs on the first Passover protect the families of God's people? What is the primary point of comparison between the first Passover lambs and what Christ did for us as our Passover Lamb?

The Last Supper as a Passover Meal

1. Preliminary Course

- Blessing of the festival day (*Kiddush*) spoken over the First Cup of wine.
- Preliminary dish of green herbs, bitter herbs, and fruit sauce.
- Serving of the meal proper (but not yet eating it) and mixing the Second Cup of wine.

2. Passover Liturgy

- The head of the family says the Passover narrative (the *haggadah*).
- Singing of Psalm 113 (called the "little *hallel*").
- Drinking the Second Cup of wine.

3. Main Meal

- A blessing is spoken over bread
- Jesus: "This is my body given for you. Do this in remembrance of me."
- Eating the meal of lamb, unleavened bread, bitter herbs.
- Blessing spoken over Third Cup of wine, (1 Corinthians 10:16).
- Jesus: "This cup is a new covenant in my blood, poured out for many (for the forgiveness of sins). Drink of it – all of you."

4. Conclusion

- Singing of Psalms 114-118 (the called "great *hallel*," Matthew 26:30).
- Blessing spoken over the Fourth Cup of wine.

Q2. Compare the annual Jewish Passover celebration meal in Jesus' day with the Christian's celebration of the Lord's Supper. Where are the similarities? Where are the differences?

Words of Institution Contain Explicit Sacrificial Terms (Matthew 26:26-28)

"While they were eating, Jesus took bread, gave thanks and broke it, and gave it to his disciples, saying, 'Take and eat; this is my body.' Then he took the cup, gave thanks and offered it to them, saying, 'Drink from it, all of you. This is my blood of the covenant, which is poured out for many for the forgiveness of sins.'" (Matthew 26:26-28)

1. Jesus associates the _____ with his own blood and then asks the disciples to drink it. (Leviticus 17:10-11; John 6:53-57.

2. Jesus identifies his blood with the institution of a _____. (Exodus 27:7-8; Jeremiah 31:31-34)

Q3. Why should the words, "This is my blood of the covenant, which is poured out for many for the forgiveness of sins" (Matthew 26:28) fill us with sorrow? Why should they fill us with joy?

---

3. Jesus links his death with the _____ sacrifice for the sins of many. (Isaiah 53:11-12)

Q4. Why is it so important to forgive those who have offended us *before* partaking of the Lord's Supper? In what sense are the Lord's Supper and unforgiveness incompatible? (Consider Matthew 26:28; 1 Corinthians 11:27; Matthew 6:14-15; 5:23-24; James 5:16.)

---

4. Jesus looks forward to the ultimate _____ in the Kingdom of God.

"I tell you, I will not drink of this fruit of the vine from now on until that day when I drink it anew with you in my Father's kingdom." (Matthew 26:29) Luke 13:28-29; 14:15; 22:30; Revelation 19:9

Q5. In what way does each celebration of the Lord's Supper anticipate a future Passover meal? (Matthew 26:29; Luke 13:28-29; 14:15; 22:30; Revelation 19:9; 1 Corinthians 11:26)

Answers to blanks: red wine, new covenant, Suffering Servant's, Passover

5. The Triumphant Lamb We Worship (Revelation 5:1-14)

The Scroll with Seven Seals (5:1-4)

axios, "pertaining to being correspondingly fitting or appropriate, worthy, fit, deserving."

The Lion Who Is the Lamb (5:5)

Genesis 49:8-12, Isaiah 11:1, 10
nikaō, "to win in the face of obstacles, be victor, conquer, overcome, prevail."

Q1. (Revelation 5:5) Why is the Lamb called "the Lion of the tribe of Judah" and "the Root of David"? What do these titles signify about him?

The Slain Lamb Standing (5:6)

"Then I saw a Lamb, looking as if it had been slain, standing in the center of the throne, encircled by the four living creatures and the elders. He had seven horns and seven eyes, which are the seven spirits of God sent out into all the earth." Revelation 5:6

Q2. (Revelation 5:6) Decode (that is, identify) each of the
following symbols that relate to the Lamb:
The lamb itself represents ....

Standing after being slain indicates ...

Horns represent ....

Eyes represent ...

The number seven carries the idea of ...

To summarize, then, the Lamb has the qualities of being of ....

Worshiping the Lamb Who Is Worthy (5:7-8)

hagios, "dedicated or consecrated to the service of God, holy,
sacred, that is, reserved for God and God's service, the holy ones,
believers, loyal followers, saints," speaking of Christians as
consecrated to God.

A Song of Redemption (5:9-10)

Q3. (Revelation 5:5) What has the Lamb done to "triumph" and
so become worthy to take the scroll and open its seals? (Hint: See
the "for" or "because" clause in 5:9 for the answer.)

A Song of Praise (5:11-14)

proskuneō, "to express in attitude or gesture one's complete
dependence on or submission to a high authority figure, (fall
down and) worship, do obeisance to, prostrate oneself before, do
reverence to...."

Philippians 2:6-11

Q4. (5:13-14) What does it tell us about the status of the Lamb that he is worshipped alongside "him who sits on the throne"?

CPSIA information can be obtained at www.ICGtesting.com
Printed in the USA
LVOW13s0152300114

371590LV00002B/503/P